# Cambodian Grrrl

## Self-Publishing In Phnom Penh

### Anne Elizabeth Moore

# Cambodian Grrrl:
# Self-Publishing in Phnom Penh

Part 1 of a 4 part series.

by Anne Elizabeth Moore

Released September 3, 2011
First printing
ISBN 978-1-934620-89-2
Cantankerous Titles #8

Cover by Esther Pearl Watson
Fonts by Ian Lynam
Designed & edited by Joe Biel

Distributed by IPG

Cantankerous Titles
PO Box 14332
Portland, OR 97293
www.cantankeroustitles.com

# Contents

In assigning class country reports, my second-grade teacher suggested I look into Cambodia. This would have been in 1976. I used an encyclopedia and did a half-assed job—not that I was in any position to find out about or comprehend what was going on there then anyway. When I got back my paper, my teacher had written on it, "You should really look into this topic more."

This is for my second-grade teacher, and the hundreds—maybe thousands—of other people around the world who have spurred on, funded, written about, or otherwise supported my work in Cambodia.

This book, and the work it describes, could not have been completed without you.

## FOREWORD

•   •   •

These young women share a world of their own with us, outside of their world, because this book is written. Learning about a culture, a way of life—how each move makes a sign that evolves into ideas and actions is not an easy task, let alone trying to pack that all in when one has to also learn the language. This book proves to us the power of writing, of recording, and the importance of giving value to each other's life.

Anne is surely a Cambodian sister. As a Cambodian woman, I am grateful that this book is published so I can learn the real lives of Cambodia's youth and their journey to a future that they can define as their own. They come from different provinces, but their hope is woven together into a shape that Cambodia will benefit from.

The horrors of genocide will remain scars in our minds forever. But the book tells us that those scars are transformed into strength and power. May the giggles, the shyness, the friendship, and love remain forever young.

Thank you, Anne for giving me a chance to look though this thin veil of your life with your Cambodian sisters. You have given me a chance to be young again, and others will share my feelings after putting down the book.

Mu Sochua, MP
Women's Rights Leader,
Sam Rainsy Party,
Cambodia

# PROLOGUE

•   •   •

Hello, my name is Anne. It is nice to meet you. This is a book I wrote. I hope you enjoy it.

You may find my name odd, particularly if you are a young Cambodian woman. But I assure you, many women in America and England and Canada are named Anne. In Mexico and Czechoslovakia and Bolivia and Italy we are called Anna. Some people, sadly, use the lesser spelling Ann. These are all common names. Many important people in history have been named this: Former Governor of Texas Ann Richards; Anne of Green Gables; Anne Frank; Anne Boleyn. Wait, those last two are terrible examples. They both died violently. How about: The pirate Anne Bonney; Um, Anne Sexton. Archeologists even recently discovered that almost half the Plesiosaurs were named Anne, or derivatives like Anne Marie, or hyphenates like Griselda-Anne. That's a completely true fact, verified by science. OK, no it's not. But if you are a young Cambodian woman, you are still looking at me funny, because you think this is all a joke. *An* means *to read* in Khmer. You will not say this out loud, though, point out that you think it is funny that a writer would be named *to read*, until I put up my hands like a *Sampea* in front of my eyes, spread them, and pretend to be engrossed in the invisible text written across my palms.

"*An*," I say. "We will have a relationship based on reading."

And then, finally, you will laugh. And my heart will rend open like a ruby red grapefruit.

•   •   •

In 1994 I sat in the kitchen of a farmhouse near Leon, Nicaragua. My hostess poured a pasty mango concoction I wasn't terribly fond of but I sipped it while she told stories about her country.

She started with a tale about when Augusto Sandino realized that Nicaragua was living under a dictatorship—one supported by a seemingly endless torrent of capital from the U.S. The soon-to-be revolutionary leader did not, she explained, pick up a hunting knife and start stabbing any American tourists he could find. She wanted to make this clear in case I had learned otherwise. No, Sandino started talking to his neighbors: What do you think about this? Are you happy? Are you eating enough? Are your children healthy?

They weren't. The Somoza family who ruled the country had overworked and underpaid farmers, business people, shopkeepers. Everyone. Most Nicaraguans weren't able to afford food, their land was being sold out from under them, they were sick, and when an earthquake hit the capital city Managua in 1972, the foreign aid sent to provide assistance was seized by the government. After 40 years of oppression, peoples' lives had only gotten worse—much worse.

By this time, Sandino himself had been killed, but the troops he had trained, farmers he fought for, and young people just coming to realize that something wasn't working in their country were calling themselves Sandinistas in his honor. Revolution is always complicated, like power and sex, but the Sandinistas perceived a clear-cut problem: The poor were still hungry and the rich were still in power. Moreover, the country was big and the problem was growing. Sandinistas could no longer go out and talk to everyone living in poverty around the nation, as was easier when the problem was more localized, and YouTube hadn't been invented yet. Writing had, so they wrote down their ideas, thoughts, experiences, and contact information, and copied and distributed these small publications— pamphlets, literature, *zines*—around the countryside.

And waited.

They waited a long time. Publishing is like that. I've been doing it since I was 11 and still find myself expecting people to be lit aflame by my ideas the second I remove them from the photocopier or get them back from the printer. But people are rarely as excited as I imagine they will be. Many let reading materials sit in stacks for hours, days, or weeks before perusing them. Good publishing—that is, the establishment and celebration of a public focused on sharing information—takes time.

Still, the Sandinistas had waited a very long time, and became concerned. They went out, again, to ask people what they thought. This time it was: What do you think about this pamphlet? What do you think about these ideas? Will they help you become happy?

And one brave farmer, changing the course of world politics with his embarrassed admission, said: We do not know how to read.

It was 1994 and I was sitting in his kitchen talking to his daughter. She explained to me how her father helped the Sandinistas develop and establish literacy programs, reading groups, and informal schools all over the country. People who had not been provided formal education, and were then kept from the possibility of educating themselves, were shown how to read about the experiences of others, and how to write down their own. Copy them. Hand them out. See what others thought. And teach them how to read, write, and publish, too.

We are taught to view this cynically, here in the U.S.: Oh, people are being indoctrinated. They are being told what to believe. Yet I was sitting in the kitchen of a woman who told me, *This is not true.* Once you learn how, you can read *anything.* You can *believe* anything. And then, most dangerous, you can *write* anything.

That other people might learn from, believe, or write about, too.

.    .    .

Thirteen years later, I had somewhat reluctantly shed the blue hair, stopped wearing slips as outwear (most of the time), and lost or broken the majority of my tiaras to the rigors of overuse or the mosh pit. I had forged a semi-legitimate career for myself in the independent publishing world, writing books and articles and putting out magazines—each in their own ways about the importance of maintaining a say in the media that represents us in a democracy. My book *Unmarketable* came out in 2007, which tracked the corporate co-optation of the cultural underground and the underground's willing participation therein—a situation to which I lost my day job, co-publishing the long-standing independent arts and culture magazine *Punk Planet.* At this point it had become clear to me that, in the U.S. at least, *democracy* was not the right of the many, but the privilege of the few. We called it democracy, but in fact many people—thousands I worked with at my magazine, talked to for my book, and knew from the dying world of independent publishing—no longer had an avenue through which they could freely express themselves. I started to become fascinated with accidental systems of oppression: Situations in which, despite claims to freedom of expression, some participants do not have access to the tools they need to communicate with each other or their government and thereby better their lives.

Cambodia had been calling itself a democracy since the mid-1990's, proven to the world despite years of civil war by UN-protected general elections that received wide international attention. Less attention-garnering are continuing reports of Cambodian journalists beaten or worse for—you know—printing verified facts about government activities and officials. In late 2007 Prime Minister Samdech Hun Sen, the former Khmer Rouge cadre voted into office during those first elections, explained these strong-arm censorship tactics by defining this elusive concept of *freedom of expression* as the freedom to say positive things about the government.

That winter, I was invited to live in the first all-women's university dormitory in Cambodia's capital city, Phnom Penh, alongside thirty-two students entering school for the first time. My knowledge of Cambodia at the time was limited to a familiarity with the phrase "Khmer Rouge atrocities," but I had heard recently that the four years this group reigned in the 1970's weren't taught in history classes, and since those who lived through them wouldn't eagerly address the traumatic time period, the mass killings that had happened in my own lifetime were rarely discussed, publicly or privately. Concrete information about the country was extremely difficult to find. There were no resources to be found on modern young female Khmer life that did not focus on sex workers, or the trials and tribulations faced by children raised in garbage dumps. The only language instruction available to me was a six-week, $5,000 video course through a local facility that catered to business and investment folk—which I could neither afford nor, considering the vocabulary that might result, see the logic in pursuing. And I only knew one person who had traveled there for purposes other than getting high.

To me, this vacuum of knowledge presented a clear project: See if the thing to which I had devoted most of my time since I was 11—promoting critical media access via print self-publishing, no longer working so well among my peers in the States—might have application in Cambodia.

•     •     •

The very first skyscraper in Cambodia—a reflective gold double monstrosity thirty-one floors taller than the tallest building in the country when it broke ground in 2007, and some ten times the height of all the other structures in Phnom Penh that could be called *tall*—was announced shortly before my first visit to the country. In a few short years, owner Yon Woo Cambodia Co., Ltd. claimed, Gold Tower 42 would extend above the dusty town, high into the clouds, providing luxury shelter and a shiny prestige to those who could afford to live there. "The One-Stop Life With Intelligent Tower," the slogan for the building reads. By its eventual completion, the road to this brilliant symbol of progress will have been as long and as riddled with potholes as Monivong Boulevard, the street on which it is being built. Since its inception, the skyscraper has been hampered by land-use concerns, an unpredictable economy, and the difficulties of assembling an engineering team in a country where virtually all the educated were killed by the Khmer Rouge thirty years beforehand in a system of social control intended to stave off exactly the kind of development Gold Tower 42 symbolizes.

Yet development—to misquote the popular U.S. bumper sticker that best approximates Cambodian pragmatism—happens. Just south of the Gold Tower 42 construction site, thirty-two daughters of Khmer Rouge regime survivors live together in the Euglossa Dormitory for University Women. Dorm residents come from all over the country, many having grown up in the abject poverty common throughout the countryside. Brilliant, feminist, well-spoken, and concerned with social justice, they are a less magnificent, more anthropomorphic, embodiment of all the Khmer Rouge sought to uproot. They will graduate from university around the same time Gold Tower 42 was planned for completion, trained for leadership roles in a nation where no jobs, mentors, or peers await them.

At least, not very many—and some of them have to be imported. At 37, I moved into Euglossa, a building full of young women half my age, intending to teach the residents self-publishing, a practice I'd been engaged in since I was a few years younger than they were. Self-publishing, though, had been easy for me to come by in the cultural underground of the U.S., where I was surrounded by other young people who made their own books, recorded their own music, and sewed their own clothes. In Cambodia, however, the government exerts massive control over expression in all forms, most of which had to be reinvented in the last 30 years anyway. Fear, censorship, and strict, traditional gender roles keep most women's concerns totally unexpressed.

On the upside, my slapdash approach bothered no one. What we think of in America as the *DIY aesthetic* is, in some parts of Southeast Asia, simply the only way to get things done. Still, even when self-expression is conceivable, it's usually thought of as *not a good idea*.

Even before I stepped off the plane then, my gender, concern for women's rights, and basic approach to living in the world marked me. Sometimes Cambodians are impressed by how well I fit in—my politeness, attentiveness, and willingness to make do with what is on offer are prized. My assertiveness, however: Not so much. As a white American woman traveling alone, I could not lose. I also would not win. At times there I am adored and at others despised, a classic tale of love and hate, set in a dust-covered town obsessed with silk and gold. My work in Cambodia is passionate, extremely productive, symbiotic, and joyful. It is also despairing, heart-wrenching, and physically dangerous. It is never what psychiatrists would call healthy. There aren't a lot of psychiatrists in Cambodia.

However, there were plenty of fortune tellers, which may offer you a few clues as to how Cambodians tend to operate. Take Gold Tower 42, for example. Since it broke ground, construction has proceeded unfettered by concerns that the national development it represents is still, well, under development. The whimsical buildings have captured the popular imagination, despite that their bawdy color and lush suites cost between 72 and 60,000 times the average worker's monthly salary. Other questions not raised about this newly emerging status symbol include the relevance of its primary investor, the South Korea-based Yon Woo Cambodia Co., Ltd. to the future economic infrastructure of the country, as well as who, exactly, will live there. The annual gross domestic product of Cambodia hovers around a very low $10 billion. (Compare to that of Illinois, which is upwards of $630 billion.) The construction of Gold Tower 42 was originally predicted to cost close to 20% of the country's GDP.

A sharp rise in the cost of building materials hit in 2008, but construction initially moved ahead anyway. The price of scaffolding had more than doubled within six months. This inflation was mirrored more popularly in increasing consumer costs of food, gas, oil, and still-not-ubiquitous electricity. Who could afford the One-Stop Life in this economy? Rumor had it, the country's political elite could. Less reliable conjecture had it that units were being sold to foreigners, lending the whole building an aura of economic surreality, wherein none of those profiting from the sales of, nor those paying out for the apartments, had any investment in or impact on the land surrounding their point of transaction. Yon Woo told the press that over half the living spaces available were sold during the first three months of construction. Sixty percent of the business units were said to be gone within the same three-month period.

So the shiny gold towers are a good barometer of change in the nation, if not actual progress. Land, for example, is one of the hottest commodities available, but rice is the second: Tension between the two has resulted in higher food costs and the loss of non-governmental food service programs to feed the poor. Elsewhere in the city, low-income housing, lakes, even the land owned by others have been and continue to be offered for sale to developers at prices that tripled between 2006 and 2008.

As a symbol of economic growth, the shiny gold mythical buildings tower above all others, an object lesson in globalization. Cambodia's reliance on foreign money—as in investors like Yon Woo, but further symbolized by the common use of the U.S. Dollar, even though there is a Cambodian currency the Riel—has crafted an unstable infrastructure, devoid of the human participants it aims to stand for, who have been physically displaced to make room for it.

From a certain distance, then, Gold Tower 42 is a charmingly brash project: Not one but two gold skyscrapers exactly in the center of a poor and dirty town. An anti-quixotic testament to the permanence of windmills. The tower's projected completion date in 2011 is not only graduation year for many first-generation Euglossa residents, but neatly coincides with the year the Cambodian National Petroleum Authority, likely alongside U.S.-based Chevron, projects it will initiate oil production on as-yet untested reserves recently discovered offshore. You had better believe this has piqued the interest of the U.S. military and U.S. investors—although U.S. aid to those living in poverty has only dwindled. Yet even this symbol of development is proving unsustainable: Construction of Gold Tower 42 was put on hold in September 2010. A 32-story building was completed in 2009—so far the tallest—and more, taller buildings are rumored, discussed, and announced.

Like the rest of Cambodia, the girls at Euglossa are desperate for any symbol, however empty, to stand for a Cambodian future that is permanent and rich and bright and strong.

•     •     •

My name is Anne. Other names have been changed to protect those I may have inadvertently misrepresented, and because the work we undertook in Cambodia is something for which others have been arrested, or worse. Still, as I remember them, and as best I can verify those I did not personally experience, the incidents occurred as I describe them. The stories herein mostly took place in or around 2007. The first traffic lights had just been installed in downtown Phnom Penh. Like Gold Tower 42, they were an exciting symbol of progress, but very few had any idea what they actually meant.

# 1

## WHERE YOU GO TODAY?

• • •

*Chandara*
"Where you go today?" Chandara asked as I clambered out of the motorcycle-driven carriage called a tuk-tuk, aggressive and challenging, but bright and flighty in a charming way. She was disarming, and you were never quite sure if she understood your sense of humor until she laughed, laughed, laughed, tossing back her long, black hair like she'd seen done in TV commercials—but not at the movies, because she'd never been to one. Part of it was language: She had only been studying English for a little over a year, a difficult skill to pick up in the Cambodian countryside where she had spent her entire life until a few short months ago. Part of it, though, was deliberate. She was smart and aggressive in a country where women were taught not to be. There were things Chandara knew. That beat before she allowed herself to respond to your joke was her way of letting you know she was special.

She certainly was. She and 31 other young women lived at the Euglossa Dormitory for University Women, a space that provided leadership skills and all-around education to a select group of social-justice minded girls entering college for the first time. Some of the new students were older than the usual age for entering university, 18; this was because the dormitory offered them their first chance to attend school and they had been waiting. Since they were rebuilt in the mid-1990s (around the same time ice came to the country) universities in Cambodia have been located only in larger cities and have not offered housing to students. Despite admissions policies that did not technically discriminate on the basis of gender, girls could not live in monasteries, where some boys resided while they attended school, and were prohibited by strong cultural mores—and often their own families—from renting apartments. Most were left with no housing options, and thus no education beyond the high-school level. Which didn't even account for the economic barriers that keep smart young people of all genders from attending any university at all. Many of the girls were so relieved and excited by the opportunity to go to college, they cried as they relayed the stories of how they came to live at Euglossa.

Being one of thirty-two future young women leaders of Cambodia was a huge responsibility in a country slightly smaller than Oklahoma where recent population estimates hovered around 14 million residents. (Oklahoma's is a quarter of that.) The national population is growing almost 2% per year, and in 2007, over half of the nation's inhabitants were under the age of 21.

It's a jarring ratio given the country's history with youth leaders, who were chosen for their easy impressionability to carry out the commands of the Khmer Rouge, under whose regime died approximately a quarter of the 1975 population. Recent estimates say as many as 2.2 million people were killed during what's come to be known as the Pol Pot years. Despite photographic and journalistic documentation of the ravages of this time period, and that every single resident of the country over the age of 30 was affected—including every single one of their parents—most of the nation's youth population didn't believe the Khmer Rouge existed.

This is one of the reasons I was drawn to the place. When I was their age, I knew more about the Khmer Rouge than some of the young women in the dorm do now. I had heard of the Killing Fields as a teenager in a movie theater 8,500 miles away, and as a girl was horrified and intrigued by the regime's willingness to give young people positions of power. Over two decades later I was no less horrified or intrigued, and I visited local genocide sites almost immediately when I came to live at Euglossa, which sits on the south side of Phnom Penh—ten blocks away from renowned torture prison Toul Sleng and nine kilometers from the Killing Fields Memorial.

I was returning from my first visit when Chandara, casting aside verb conjugations and any sense of respect her culture demanded she harbor for elders, wanted to know where I go today. It was Christmas Day, an event I viewed with a cynicism in the States that was only amplified here. Phnom Penh was in the midst of its first city-wide acknowledgment of the holiday, by way of what was referred to as the traditional Christmas Sale. Given the other options, I couldn't think of a more appropriate way to spend a day reflecting on the meaning of global peace than by visiting the memorial site. The nine-kilometer journey had only taken half an hour by motorcycle-drawn carriage, but it felt significant. This so-called Killing Field was arguably the Khmer Rouge's most infamous accomplishment: A suburban farm devoted to the mass execution of enemies of the state, although similar mass graves spread throughout the entire country, and more continue to be discovered. The Killing Fields Memorial wasn't, at the time, really a museum; neither was it exclusively a memorial. It was simply raw proof, a still-under-excavation site owned by a Japanese corporation and informally staffed by locals who hung around the front gate charging the exorbitant price of a couple bucks for tours. My naked fascination embarrassed me: I had wanted to go there for 23 years. And today I had done it.

"Where you go today?!" Chandara insisted again, louder, when I didn't respond, likely more concerned that I had misunderstood her pronunciation than that I was ignoring her. One does not ignore Chandara.

"Oh, *Cheung Eck*," I explained hesitatingly, using the Khmer name for the memorial. Together Chandara and I spoke Khmenglish, a mixture of languages that eliminates helper verbs and most articles, adds S's to words that don't need them. I continued. "It was hard. I am sad now. *Khnyom kartok*," I said.

I expected an emotional torrent from her, or a roadblock. An expression of rage or sympathy. At least a knowing look. I had witnessed something revelatory and horrifying about her past, her culture, her people. She had a right to claim it from me. To put me in my place as a foreigner, as white, as inexperienced. As, on this matter, stupid. Which I was. I awaited her outburst.

The position I was standing back to ensure her—the privilege of outrage, her birthright—was one I was familiar with. I have lived on several reservations in South Dakota and unless you have, too, you cannot tell me what Native American Indian reservations are like, really. If, like me, you present as white and middle class, I will query you on your ethnic heritage and personal background if you crack genocide jokes on Thanksgiving, or blithely refer to Indian Time. The same principle applied here: Chandara deserved the right to narrate her lived experience.

"What is it?" She asked.

I blamed my Khmer pronunciation for her failure to understand. "Umm, the Killing Fields?"

"Uh huh," she said. Knowing. Only knowing those words, though. "What is it?" She repeated.

I had lived with her for nearly a month by then, and Chandara *was* smarter than most Cambodian teenagers. Still, her blank expression and continued confusion in response to my hurried explanation indicated that she had never heard of the Killing Fields. She could not claim her own history. Not because she did not have the skills or the urge or the language to do so, but because she did not know it.

And I wasn't prepared to explain it to her.

•   •   •

## Welcome to Phnom Penh

Among the many features both pleasing and perilous the Cambodian capital sports, the grid system I grew accustomed to in Chicago is most certainly not among them. City planning, the way I conceive of it, is not prized here. Even on the Internet, where you can find everything, some map sites do not render Phnom Penh, instead supplying the phrase "Image not available." The city has been the capital of Cambodia several times in recent centuries—the modern nation can be traced back to around the year 800—but since 1866, with one notable exception, it has remained the permanent seat of government.

The haphazard placement of streets connecting temples to lakes to markets to the Mekong was wrestled into some semblance of Western-minded order when French city planners added canals, built roads, and established ports in the 1880s—an order only given over again to entropy 95 years later when the town was emptied at gunpoint by the Khmer Rouge and left vacant for four years. In the 1990s, the city began to rebuild, but the vast majority of concentric streets that form a large circle around the center of the city still don't have names. Not to worry: Some have numbers, it's just that they occasionally have the same numbers as streets on the other side of town, or are known more popularly by charming markers like Try Samphea's house. As a foreigner, of course, you neither know where Try Samphea lives, nor could you guess what his family's abode might look like even if you knew something about him. Still, you are always welcome to ask, if you have grasped the language, or if you are up for the comedy of receiving the possible answer, *It is near Vann Sokchea's house.*

Another barrier westerners may stumble across while searching out any given location will be the house-numbering system. This, at least, contains a basic comprehensible logic, although one not at all founded on the consecutive order of numbers. House numbers are chosen for auspicious occasions, or for luck, or because they simply have good sounds. Thus a house 8 may well be next door to house 53, across the street from number 187, which is likely next door to a second house 187, and possibly a third.

Yet it is one thing to know this in advance: It is another to attempt to maneuver through it. So I balked, at first, when an acquaintance had offered to pick me up at the airport, and then agreed. My idea of urban adventuring relies fairly heavily on taxi drivers knowing their way around town, communication with locals who discern locations from addresses, and the existence of maps. The only clues I had to my destination were scrawled directions the Euglossa foundation director had told me over the phone before my flight:

1. Go toward the lake. (The *other* lake, the director had stressed.)

2. Find Street 147. You will see a furniture store next to a coffeeshop, which will be next to another furniture store. Take a right.

3. This is also Street 147, and all the streets now off the road you just took are called Street 147 as well. In about 500 meters, take a left.

4. Across from the people sleeping in front of the third furniture store is a gate. Ring the bell. It is house number 65.

These directions made little sense to my acquaintance, and none whatsoever to my taxicab driver, but my eagle eye for furniture stores kicked in at just the right moment and there I found myself: The Euglossa Dormitory for University Women.

From the street, I could see: Euglossa was a narrow, three-story building marked by a lopsided Apsara, a locked gate, and an armed guard. From the balcony you could peer into a courtyard and spy on the family to the east, if you wanted to. Along with their usually pantsless toddler, they lived in a ramshackle tin-roof thing, and their job was acquiring gasoline from the Vietnamese and selling it illegally. This explained the very large pile of plastic gas canisters thrown haplessly into the corner of their dirt enclosure. To the west was a brothel. No windows face their building, so you couldn't see inside, but the open window policy would later allow me to hear everything the residents did, day and night. And they did a lot.

So serene, deferential, and marked was the Euglossa dorm from its neighbor buildings that it could have been a guest house, the more personable version of a hotel available for travelers, and it did in fact look like the modestly opulent one just a few meters down the dirt path, on another of the streets known as Street 147. But Euglossa was not a guest house. It was a girl explosion—a conundrum of energy and enthusiasm and giggling and affection and gratitude and stubbornness.

Here it was, in front of me.

•   •   •

## Roomful of Puppies

Like walking into a room you didn't know would be filled waist-high with puppies: Girls, jumping, squealing, giggling, holding your hand, hugging and tugging and every one with eyes wider and more heartbreakingly beautiful than the last. Every one in a silly T-shirt with some weird misspelling, every one so ready and charming and enthusiastic that you want to adopt them all. Really, you do. You want to bring them home, all thirty-two of them, and a small part of your heart clicks into place and you know that this is like love. You think, Oh. It was all preparation for this. The greatest affairs of my life, my parents, my closest friends—were just practice. This is what love is supposed to be. These girls are gushing and chattering and singing and pink—really, they are!—and you barely notice because you haven't understood a word yet, but the sensation, it is a melting thing, and when you think of this moment even years later you want to cry and laugh, you will feel ashamed and bold, confused and enlightened. And you will wish, more than anything, that you could be in that moment again.

And I am: The bustle of hugs, the excited clamor, and suddenly one girl was holding my hand sweetly while the rest are shouting, laughing, asking questions. Even now my heart skips a beat. "You are my roommate," the girl said. "Do you know my name?"

She had a rounded face and clear eyes and black razor-straight hair. She was speaking English. I had never seen her before in my life. I did not even know what sorts of words make names in this language. In fact, I could hardly distinguish the characters that make up the alphabet. They seemed too elaborate, too pretty, to have meaning. I stalled for time.

"Um, do you know mine?" I asked her.

"Anne," she said. "It means to read in Khmer."

"Oh." I was impressed. "I don't know yours."

"Socheat," she said. "But the people who love me call me Amoun."

"Amoun," I repeated.

Then Amoun took me upstairs and showed me the three by four meter room I would live in with three teenagers for two months. I got the bottom bunk.

•     •     •

*I Kind of Fear That My Legacy Will be the High Five*

After a nap and some fast unpacking—I shared a closet with a 17-year-old girl who grew up in abject poverty, so brought few clothes—I emerged from my room to discover: A party! A good old-fashioned one with food and singing and a little bit of dancing. Everything moved at excitable puppy pace, and the girls were all there plus the dorm staff plus many travelers and so! Much! Giggling!

We sang. We ate spaghetti. We played with each other's hair.

An American visitor, an older white man, performed a horrible version of the Apsara. This traditional ballet relies on sure balance, tiny limbs, total grace, and extensive training. Importantly, it was not recommended for aging white dudes. It sent the girls into peals of giggles. Everything else did, too. A frog croak, on the wall, was almost as funny.

"I am so happy," many of the girls said to me, drawing out each syllable of the last word as if it were a translation from the Khmer: *Hap Py*. "It is so wonderful to have you here." And it was wonderful to be there.

It was fun, so I said to one of the girls, "This is fun."

"Funny?" She asked, which started another fit of giggles. She said it like: *Fun Ny?*, followed by laughter. Even the word funny, to these young women, was enough for their keen sense of humor to go on for hours.

"No," I corrected. "Fun." The point of that word gets lost quickly pretty quickly when you repeat it emphatically, let me tell you. Blank stare. "I enjoy it?" I said. Still nothing. Hmm. I resorted to the concept they understood: "I am happy."

"Good." I heard in response. "We are all happy."

Cambodians understand happiness. Being happy is a popular theme in art and literature, second only to being sad, and bested only by being in love. But fun represents a problem—the levity brought on by deliberately non-productive activity. "What is to be accomplished, with fun?" the girls would ask me later.

But you understand: The party was fun. Even if I was so tired I forgot the two words of Khmer that I was able to pick up during the day—*Thank you* is *Akun* and *Hello* is . . . Oh, damn. I remembered exactly one of the girls' names. They think Americans dumb for not knowing them, and who can blame them? They are right. They have no trouble with our names. Yet there are a great many girls, and although they are each exceedingly unique and hilarious, the fact was that not a one of them was named any single thing I have ever heard of before. So I wasn't just learning a new person, I was learning an entirely new language for people. But you understand.

Eventually, the party streams diverted into one older, languid pool of satisfied but exhausted Americans, and one still-rushing river of Cambodian girl enthusiasm; as I perhaps have made clear, my energy and manner of dress runs, according to my professional colleagues, disappointingly toward the latter. I joined the group of girls. They sat in a circle, singing quietly, laughing, playing paddy-cake-like games with their hands. Excuses to touch each other. They call themselves sisters, but they are closer than that.

The entirely new language for girls, once I mastered it, included the aforementioned Amoun, who moved immediately, wordlessly aside when I approached, welcoming me again, assuming my interest in sitting next to her. To my left sat Leung, a wide-faced girl who betrayed a very slight lisp when speaking. Overweight by Cambodian standards—healthy by American—Leung's singing voice was the reason her sisters in the dorm didn't tease her, despite the raw-bone look they preferred in each other. Her voice was soul-jerking, world-splitting, devastating. Her frequent and often unplanned performances were made poignant by her chosen repertoire of songs about the romantic love felt by young girls who would never marry, stupid girls whose place in the world was only redeemed by their ability to fall in love, and girls who, both young and stupid, were thrown aside by careless boys, who were just being boys. The injustice she carried around with her in the form of these memorized songs caused Leung's nerves to run high, and she was apt to lose patience and snap at her sisters, perceiving judgment when there was none. Some clearly feared her sharp tongue.

She was seated next to Lili, the second of my roommates, who had chosen a reasonable course of study for a nation in the midst of rebuilding an economic infrastructure: Accounting. She had also decided to pursue three languages, and these are what may, in the end, make her employable: She could move to England, the U.S., Canada, Japan, or any of the French-speaking nations and account. In her own country, such employment, for young women, was rare. But Lili's real talent was a wicked sense of humor, a teasing manner so vicious that, next to Leung, she did not speak. She quietly made funny faces so her sister could not get angry. I adored her immediately, silently repeating her name over and over and memorizing what she looked like: Her hair was thicker and wavier then most of her sisters, her eyes darker and faster, her mouth quicker to laugh. Kimlong, next to her, was usually the first to catch Lili's jokes. Her heart was free, and she was open to any new experience. She couldn't see Lili's actions there in the circle, so she led the group in activities, jumping up and play-acting when a visual was called for; straightening her spine and projecting when a new song necessary, always with a gusto that seemed to indicate, *I have never cared so much about anything in my entire short life.*

Amara was next, dark and quiet and stunningly beautiful. She never bothered to practice her English and had no patience for my Khmer, so we would communicate through a vocabulary built mostly around the word "love."

Quieter, and to Amara's left, was Sosaryna. A law student with well-practiced English, Sosaryna was taken, always, to be the smartest in the group. A born leader with an easy, confident smile. I was immediately suspicious of the beautiful, successful teen. Which confused: Such girls in the States I would look at and think, "Haven't you ever suffered? Don't you have the faintest idea how the world works?" But Sosaryna's father was a soldier in the protracted civil war, and while a sense of privilege may have grown from her slightly elevated class status, one could not accuse her of not knowing about the workings of the world. She was Cambodian.

Sosaryna's polar opposite seated next to her was Dina Sun, a tall quiet girl, a charming intellectual one feigning shyness. She was perpetually a little bit sad, which fueled her romantic tendencies, and somehow fulfilled all of my preconceived notions of what second-generation genocide survivors might be like: Untrusting, dampened, distracted. I shouldn't tell you this now, I should wait until you know me better, but waiting won't make it any less true: Dina Sun almost repulsed me. I could not stand, yet fully empathized with, her inability to adapt. So unlike her best friend Sotheary, who in turn, fulfilled all of my notions about what an American Teen was like—except she was Cambodian. Frivolous, silly, jokey, enamored of the color pink, and more than willing to pull one over on someone if it seemed funny to her, Sotheary could be dropped into the center of any sitcom and steal the hearts of the viewing audience with clever repartee. In an American sitcom, she would be the star, and Dina Sun's occasional morose quips would make her the foil. But we were not in an American sitcom. No: Things will not get worked out neatly here. Dina Sun, and the sorrow she laid at your feet openly, and every day—all of it, so much of it—these are the interstitials, the commercials always at the ready when the action stops or the scene changes. Dina Sun made me uncomfortable because she constantly reminded me I was in Cambodia.

Someone cracked a loud joke, another song was sung, a surprising fete impressed me, and then it happened. It may have been unforgiveable: I raised my right hand high above my head, looked sure to strike the young person in front of me, and said—nay, demanded—"High five."

I should mention that I was never, like, a sports fan. I also don't enjoy arena rock, don't drink beers out of cans and then crush them to my forehead, and I have never once gone "Duuuuude" appreciatively after someone else made an oppressive sexual comment about a pleasant-looking woman on the street. I am, however, a devotee of the high five as a casual greeting, as a sort of, *Hooray! You're here now! Which is so great! Even though we are at work!* Sometimes even as a stand in for a *Congratulations on that great news! I bought you a present!*, and even more occasionally as a way of saying, *You know what? I am walking by you and having a bit of a crappy day. So let's fake it with this high five business 'til we make it, shall we?* But what I remember from that night was that one of the girls did something spectacular, and I responded by saying, "High five!" And holding my hand up as if I were about to cheerily smash her face in. And then I had to explain myself and teach them the high five.

This is never easy. You, yourselves, probably know that there are tricks to the high five. You have to be pretty confident to make it work, not to mention have upper body strength and aim. Pretty quickly several of the girls were doing good high fives, which as the readers at home are aware, is always preceded by the announcement, "High five!" At one point in the evening there were so many high fives going on that one of the American women seated across the courtyard, gaily chatting with the older crowd, came over and shook her head mournfully at me. "I'm not even sure I want to know where this is going," she said.

Where it was going was nowhere, fast: Quickly, the concept of the high five devolved from an action to an expression. By dessert, it had become little more than a salutation. "High five," Amoun said to me pleasantly as she sat down, balancing both a bowl and a water bottle. No intention of slapping me anything.

Day one: I'd had an impact on Cambodian culture, and it was the high five. Great.

•     •     •

## Bong

"Bong?" A woman asked me.

As I usually do when I am faced with something I do not understand, I panicked inwardly, and probably looked angry. She was calling me *sister*, but I could not be expected to know this yet. *I am a stupid American!* I screamed inwardly. *I have not yet had my coffee! I have been up since 2! I do not know the name of the women who sleeps above me, nor can I communicate with her in any way!* I was turning into a raving lunatic. It was my first morning in Phnom Penh. I was ready to go home.

But in a vague, pan-Euro accent, I requested, "Kah-Fe?" And she returned a moment later with iced, bitter drink. It was a small victory, but I celebrated by loading my glass up with sugar and grossly overtipping her.

Then I sat in the cafe in a wooden straight-backed chair next to a shiny rosewood table and sipped my coffee. Next to me, of course, was a furniture shop.

I evaluated the last 24 hours and thought to myself: *You came here to make zines?*

.　　.　　.

## But I Need to Explain

As if to welcome me, the girls have been speaking in English when they are within earshot, and sometimes even when they are not. From down the hall I can occasionally hear a sweet, sweet, "Hello, my love," or similar: They are incurably romantic, as if the physical incarnations of a Khmer/Disney Hybrid Princess. Living in close quarters to such a thick frosting of charm and kindliness might occasionally make you say to yourself, "Oh barf."

Two of the worst offenders are my roommates, Amara and Lili. The cynical part of me that cannot help but read romance as tied to consumerism, that looks for the nearest exit when a new young person expresses her true and undying love for me, was triggered every few moments by their giggling coos, smiling cheery support, occasional queries about how studying, classes, or dinner are proceeding. "Oh barf," the back of my mind responds automatically. Yet this was not uncommon, this unbounded affection. Probably not for anyone who steps off a plane in Cambodia.

"I have a dream about you," one of the girls told me, cheerfully awake at 6 a.m. and happily dusting the computer room where I was taking notes. "You give one thing to me, and that is love." She said. It was ridiculous, sure. But it was a dream that was true, I told her.

Note in contrast that Amara was studying to be a lawyer—Kimlong and Sosaryna too—in a country that rates poorly in all annual corruption indices. Rule of Law, the notion that a legal system applies to all citizens of any governed body, is not commonly understood to exist in Cambodia, a factor considered among the most significant when accounting for national corruption. Particular problem areas have been noted in the legal system: Appeals may not be resolved in a timely manner or for a reasonable cost; judgments within the legal system do not necessarily follow written law; judicial decisions are not always enforced by the state; the state holds enormous influence over judges; judicial decisions often seem open to racial and ethnic bias; women, the poor, and individuals who live away from city centers do not have full access to the judicial system; and small businesses and citizens earning the median yearly income cannot always afford to bring a case to court. The on-the-books fees are not the problem here—unofficial payments are. So studying the law in Cambodia was something of a massive undertaking. An affront, already, to the way things work.

Of particular concern to the law students in Euglossa was the acknowledgement that women simply don't access the legal system. Not that they are legally banned from doing so, of course. But they neither have knowledge of their legal rights or the judicial system at large, nor do they see the law as an effective response to issues such as, for example, domestic violence.

My theory is, a romantic world view here was not simply boy-craziness made universal, and it isn't a jarring incongruity on a young woman who will soon bedeck herself almost exclusively in power suits. In Cambodia, a heartfelt belief that love can conquer all challenges was simply a survival skill for any would-be lawyer. Or for that matter, any accountant, teacher, or engineer.

2

## PARENT'S DAY

•   •   •

*Year Zero*
"I've been here since the beginning," Ms. Sonrith Channy told me. "I've been here since Year Zero."

The girls call her Ms. Channy as a sign of respect. She was the Euglossa dorm manager, so her role was to mentor and inspire the next generation of women leaders in Cambodia. This would be enough of a task for someone who grew up in middle-class comfort during peacetime. But Ms. Channy was seven years old when the Khmer Rouge marched all the residents of Phnom Penh out of the city, forcing the nation into an ill-planned agrarian utopia that ended in mass death. I asked her to tell me her story because she was exactly one year older than I was.

"I was born in 1969," She said. "During that time my family was middle class, Cambodian middle class. My father was working with the government and my mother, she stayed at home and had a small business. Our family lived very good and peacefully. But in 1975, the Khmer Rouge regime started in Cambodia and Pol Pot said, everyone should go out to the countryside. So my family also must go out, like other people in Phnom Penh. We were living near Psar Tmein market. Central Market. And we went to Kampung Cham province. During Pol Pot regime, I would like to say: Very dark period for Cambodian people. All Cambodian people, not only my family. I found a very difficult life there because they divided children separately in a group, mothers in the group of mothers, father in the group of fathers. That means it was very difficult to meet each other. For years."

Ms. Channy sat erectly, with her long silk skirt properly tucked around her, legs uncrossed, crisp white shirt uncanny in the broiling afternoon heat. A hidden psychology was at work in a figure like this. When Ms. Channy caught herself expressing too much pain, she reared back into a presentation of facts.

"Now I would like to go back to the history of my family," she said. "My father was a Buddhist monk. When I grew up I was interreligious because my mother, she is a Christian. She was born in a Christian family. My grandmother was French and my grandfather was Cambodian Chinese. They lived in Cambodia and make a business, a big business, in the Norodom Sihanouk regime. But after that, my father got married with my mother and moved to live in Phnom Penh.

"I was born in Phnom Penh. Every day, when I was in childhood, my father, he used to say about the history of Buddhism. So to me, as a Cambodian woman, I belong to father. I'm a Buddhist. But I do respect all religions. During Pol Pot time, my father, he make himself like stupid people. He worked for government, before. So: Very danger. And when Pol Pot come, sometimes he cried, sometimes he laughed, sometimes he say something like a bird. Sometimes he sing a song. And if the Khmer Rouge ask him to do something, he do. But if they ask him, 'Do you know some English, or some French?' He said, 'No. I don't know. What's French? What's English?' It was scary, because he had long hair, and all the children run after him. Me too! I ran after him! Tease him. Chase him. My mother, she was crying, every time. She thought my father had become stupid. Crazy. He did not tell anyone.

"After Pol Pot, he become normal again. He become smarter. My mother asked him, 'Why you become normal now?' He said, 'I made my body become stupid and crazy during Pol Pot regime. Otherwise they would kill me.'

"I was seven years old. Separated from my parents right away, in April, 1975. The period of the moving from Phnom Penh to Kampung Cham province was about two months by foot, by walking. And there, they separated us. During Pol Pot time, very hard because they don't allow us to meet each other, and then they provide food—very little. Working hard, eating less.

"They took me to a children group and then they said, 'If you don't work today, we don't have food for today.' So they build a canal and everyone bring the land to fill for the canal—for water. So you can imagine, this work is very difficult for the children like me. During that time I was only seven years old! And I'd never been hard working like this before! So at that time, I was crying because I don't know how to bring the land upstairs."

Transporting the earth, she means: Up the bamboo structures featuring steps sometimes as tall as she was. Having killed most trained engineers, urban planners, and architects—scaring the remainder into silence—the Khmer Rouge were fond of attempting sophisticated construction projects with little but vague memories and pictures in books to go on. Structures were supported with mud built up from rice paddy walls and rickety ladders. Adults complain of them nowadays too. And then they cut the food.

"They don't give three meals," she continued. "One year into Pol Pot regime, they didn't make enough rice. The point of regime, of revolution was: Triple rice production. Three times amount of rice. So they keep it for themselves, don't feed the people. Give back to Chinese in owe for guns. I was, how you say, very sick. Very sick, I nearly died. Someone have kind heart, come to my mother far away from there and told to my mother, 'Oh, your daughter nearly die because of no food.' My mother come to visit the children's organization—I can say it like this? Children's organization—and they say to her, 'Oh, your daughter is very lazy. Don't work. And now, no food, and after that, sick.'

"So my mother just kept quiet because during Pol Pot regime, no one can say something against Angkar. You know, the big one." Ms. Channy meant: The Khmer Rouge leaders never called themselves Khmer Rouge. They called themselves and their superiors *Angkar*, pronounced like this: Ang*k*a. It means association, organization. The feeling it compels is one of ubiquitous fear.

She continued, "My mother cried and bought some food, like dried fish and small rice, but I did not take it because I was very sick—nearly dead. But this period passed. I got healthy and got better and better. I don't know why. Maybe God helped me. After that, I remember one time I saw a lot of children studying my language under the mango tree. I also sit there under the mango tree and I just repeat. And the Pol Pot members told me that, 'Oh, you are smart, you remember everything. You are the new student, but you remember everything. So please come to teach them.'"

"New student," Ms. Channy repeated, and explained in her own way that, to facilitate the transformation of society to its agrarian ideal, Angkar divided the Cambodian population into two groups: New people, who were urban, educated, or otherwise tainted by capitalism; and everyone else. This latter group, sometimes called old people, but often just unmarked, resided in villages, farmed in the traditional manner, and lived in a society that closely represented what the Khmer Rouge wanted to enforce nationally. It achieved a balance of power rare in the modern world: Calling something 'new' in Cambodia still means it is a little bit distasteful and largely unwelcome.

"I said, 'No! I can't teach them.'" Ms. Channy was not just responding to the fear she felt being singled out as a seven-year-old, separated from her parents and forced to labor in starvation. She was responding to the position of leadership she was being offered in the Angkar.

"He said, 'No. You teach them.' The Khmer Rouge leader handed me some papers and said, 'When I ask you to give the paper to the students, you please distribute them.' And during that time, I hid one. I keep one for myself."

She laughed, and added: "But I scared, too. He is not a big person, but he is older than me, maybe five or eight years. I have a pencil, but I feel very scared. So I very respectfully tell him, 'Teacher. May I have this piece of paper, and this piece of pencil?' He said, 'Of course! Why not? You are also included in this class, under the mango tree.'

"This piece of paper very meaningful to my learning. I write on it and study. Unfortunately, the class start only one week and then finish. Why? You know, they were very clever. They wanted to move all the children in the village to another village, where they wanted us to look after the birds. Because in the corn field there was a lot of birds who would eat the corn. The canal was finished, too.

"So the leaders said, 'OK. Everybody go to the other village.' It was also in Kampong Cham, but we were very lucky because we just were looking after the birds. So, it's a long story, but three years. . . . I do not want to say."

Ms. Channy paused. She never filled in for me what happened over those three years, never again would mention even that she had lived them. She started again, formally. Tucking her skirt about her, asssuring the smoothness of her crisp, white top. "I would like to continue my life after 1979. After Pol Pot regime." She said. "When Vietnam soldiers come to Cambodia in 1979, all organization in Pol Pot regime said, 'You are free. You can go to your family.'

"So I met my family in the village. It took only one week to walk back home. But not all the orphans came successfully to meet each other, because some family was killed during that time. They killed parents, killed daughter, killed sister, like that. My family, I lost my grandparents. Then after 1979, we come back to Phnom Penh. We stay at my house." She looked at me instead of explaining that many *didn't* stay in their former homes. After the Vietnamese invasion, the notion of property ownership was strained. Even beforehand, the Khmer Rouge had changed and abolished home ownership and property rights laws, and by the time the regime was ousted, everything was confused. Your political beliefs dictated what you felt you had a right to; age and memory further skewed any sense of entitlement. The Vietnamese government at one point decreed that if you lived in a residence, it was yours.

"My father," Ms. Channy continued, "He had some knowledge. He know how to work in the office. He had worked for government before. Some people come to him, asked him, 'Now we want to announce for the people who have some knowledge to start a new Cambodian government.' My father was afraid because we did not know. Would they kill new government too? He worked in the government as the chief of the district. I start in school in the first grade. I was older than them. The youngest one was about 6 years old. I was maybe 10, 11. But tall, also. Tall and thin."

"My father said, I want you to study hard. Please study with me. Mathematics, physics, history, French. So in only one year I passed three grades. So the teacher boosts me from one grade to the fourth grade. It was very hard, because, like the other children, I want to play. During that time I was very angry with him. Now I am grateful. My family during that time was very poor. No salary in the new government. They give rice. There wasn't money."

The Khmer Rouge had destroyed the old currency but failed to implement a new one before the Angkar was overthrown. *There was no Cambodian currency.* This isn't a metaphor for poverty: There was no such thing as money.

Instead, "they give rice and some expired milk from Russia," Ms. Channy said. "We didn't know. Now I know: Expired food. Because the cans still stand at my house. They expired around 1970. But we ate in 1979 or 1980. Not good quality to our body.

"In high school, I was the youngest one in the class. But I was class leader. Why, I don't know. Maybe the teacher thought it was easy to use me. He appointed me to be a class leader, and then every classmate was not happy with me.

"Later, in 1983, I was voted to be a leader *of school*, not class. But the dean of the school came to me and said, 'You are a girl. There is a man who should have this job and you should be a team leader.' I was very angry with him. I said, 'Why? This is the result from the vote!' He said, 'I don't know why that happened. But you are a woman.'

"I asked him, 'Please compare the result of study, the appearance, count the vote again.'

"He said, 'Oh Channy, you want me to compare. But I did already. He is a man. You are a woman.'" In the U.S., remember, Geraldine Ferraro was just then gearing up for this same debate. American schoolgirls like myself were told that her bid for the vice presidency meant sexism had been eradicated, that women could do anything.

"Everyone was very angry who was my supporter. This was many people, because they voted for me. So the new leader of the school, he said, 'You look after discipline in this school.' I was called team leader, but I do everything. Everything that happened then, he said, 'Up to you. You decide.' Because he was lazy.

"Another reason, his house was very far from the school. He said, 'Everything that has a big responsibility for the school, you should ask Channy, because Channy lives near the school.' I did not have title, and I did not have power, but I have much responsibility. This is what I think about being Cambodian woman."

She paused, looked at me piercingly. What was not stated in Cambodia was as important as what was. She communicated clearly, although not verbally: Women in Cambodia work, her gaze said. But they will never be acknowledged for it.

I did not disbelieve her. The same thing happened in the U.S.

"So in 1986 I passed my high school examination and I received a scholarship to go to Russia. The problem is the economy in my family: Not good. My parents, especially my father, were very worried because we didn't have any money to pay for me to go abroad. But my mom had a good solution. At that time, we had a piglet of about 20 kilos. My father sell the pig. But you know, a 20 kilogram pig can be exchanged for only one jean. And a small, small suitcase. White. But I was very happy.

"But in the market, my father heard from people. They tell him, 'It's not good for girls to go abroad.' He say to me, 'I want you to not go, to stop thinking about it.' He wanted to see my passport. But I said, 'No.' I had heard from the organizer if I do not have the passport, I cannot go. So I hide the passport.

"After that I heard my mother and my father arguing. I heard my mother say, 'I want her to go. I believe in my daughter. If you don't believe, OK. I have pregnant her, I fit her in closer than you, OK. If you don't believe in my daughter, OK.'

"He said, 'I believe, but I am worried.'

"My mother said, 'How do you lead a district but you don't encourage your daughter?' This touched my heart. My father go away. I brought my mother a glass of water and said, 'Mother, thank you for your support.' I also was crying. She said, 'We are body woman, but the heart not woman. We are stronger than that. So please go. I have confidence in you.'

"I got a lot of bad words from my neighbors. Because this is the first time in history that a girl planned to go abroad to study for seven and a half years. They called our family the new villager. Even after the Pol Pot regime, all of them are old villagers, but we are new villagers. They said, 'You are the new villagers and you want to make history.' One woman said, 'Your daughter will come back with a baby but no husband.' This is very critical to Khmer culture, this point. A baby but no husband mean, you are dirty. Worthless. You should die.

"So I was very angry with her. But my mother said, 'We will see.' So I spent almost eight years in Russia. My life completely changed.

"One thing I found very difficult was money management. When I was living with my family in Cambodia I had no problem, because everything I want to have, I just ask money from my mother. But in Russia I had a scholarship. They gave me 19 Rubles per month. Small. The first time I spent all money on chocolate because I never ate chocolate. When I ate chocolate, it seemed good to me. So one month, I just ate chocolate. But my body's temperature became higher, every day. I prayed: Please end the month, please end the month. Because I want to eat something else besides chocolate. So after that, I know how to manage money. I was 17 years old.

"I thought maybe I was beautiful, because every single day, someone would come to my room. An African, Russian, a Cambodian. But my mother had warned me. Cambodian people cannot do anything until they are married. And those people are just coming to be your boyfriend. I did not want my neighbor to have true.

"Another problem: Language. Russian language, I don't know. I just know *Spasiba*. I solved the economic problem. I allocated money for food, for transportation. And for the people who want to disturb, I feel what my mother said, I feel what the people in the village said. And I just smiled. And eventually the people who come to me, they learn. I will not pregnant. But the language—they had me sharing a room with three Russian ladies. They were older than me by about three or five years. They were very strong. At the time I have a problem with my hair because it is very long, and it always fall out with the new climate. My roommates were very angry with me. At first I didn't have words to explain in Russian, because I don't know. When they say, *your hair*, in Russian, I say *Spasiba. Thank you.*"

Ms Channy laughed, hard, at her own joke before continuing. "Then I try to show that, I don't want the hair to fall. Who wants? After five or six months, we become friends. I can tell you that my first year in Russia was no good, because the language. Mathematic, I can do it because of the formula. But when they say, 'Describe,' I cannot describe. But about six months into my second year, I learn.

"I started studying meteorology in 1987. I did not choose meteorology. When I got a scholarship, the government chose. How many people go to this subject, how many go to this. I don't know how they choose.

"Cambodians start corruption from that period, I think. Because I observe that children of relatives have received very good subject. My father only a district chief. He did not have a lot of power with them.

"I like meteorology, but if I had my choice I would want to study governmental policy. I want to be a diplomat but I don't have chance. So in 1993 I come back to Phnom Penh, to my country. They sent me to work with the Ministry of Water Resources and Meteorology. I was chief of the Office of Weather Forecasting. I go to teach on environmental management at the university. I teach on Saturday. So I have experience teaching, have opportunity to go abroad. But in 1996, my family's economy very poor, very terrible, so I thought that I should work part time with some organization.

"So I find the announcement for a job, a U.N. food program wants a food monitor. It said, 'Women are encouraged to apply.' So I apply and the interviewer said, 'Come to work.' His name was Mr. Henning. He said, 'Work with me in the Prey Veng province. Your salary as a food monitor will start from $420 U.S.D. per month.' It was a high salary because I have a Masters, and at the U.N. they respect the degree. So I told the director at the ministry, she was my friend: 'I want to earn some money.' She said, 'You please go, but if the boss contact me, I contact you.'

"So at that time, I was in charge of three district, working with orphanages, providing the food. I worked there two years, and then the Ministry of Water Resources said, 'Where are you? Please come back to work. Otherwise they will dismiss you from the government.' The director had called to me. And I completely told Mr. Henning, I must leave. I had a different job for two years before the government ask about me."

I asked Ms. Channy, "Were you getting paid for both jobs?" And she smiled.

"The corruption." She said. "It is terrible."

When she finally left government work, Ms. Channy told me, she found an ad. Wanted: Woman leader. New dormitory.

Ms. Channy applied.

•     •     •

## Parents' Day

A few days into my stay at Euglossa, the students' parents gathered from all corners of the country. Because the country's about the same size as Illinois, it didn't strike me as a terribly big deal to travel any distance within it until I saw them pulling up, two or three to a moto, carrying in their laps or between their legs enormous bags of the unique kind of rice that the family grows at home, and that their daughter especially loves—in fifty or hundred pound bags. It would line the walls of the dorm's storage area for months.

The purpose of Parents' Day was to hold a special ceremony to thank the parents for letting their daughters come live in the dormitory. Which, again, if you're still thinking about Illinois won't seem such a big deal until you understand that nothing in Cambodian history has given them reason to believe it's a good idea for girls to go off and live together away from home.

The overwhelming beauty and love and happiness so radiating from the older generation had allowed me to completely forget that these girls' own parents *did* leave home at some point, at a very early age. At an age they weren't ready to. They had been uprooted, like Ms. Channy, like the rest of the nation, moved somewhere across the country, packed into labor camps, separated from parents and sent to live with randoms, maybe, or other kids.

The Khmer Rouge plan was to triple rice production in the country by both increasing labor and decreasing use, overworking and underfeeding the populace until almost a quarter died. Their siblings died, their parents, their friends. Survivors were forced into marriages to sever blood relations and enforce an allegiance only to the regime.

Parents—their parents, all parents—were deemed inherently capitalist. Children—now parents of the children I lived with—were considered ripe for education, ready to transform society into an agrarian utopia. These lessons were not merely instructed. They were memorized in rote recitation sessions of strings of repeated aphorisms. They were backed up by beatings, threats, and years of what, under normal circumstances, we would consider torture. Public executions. Disappearances. There were hundreds of imaginable reasons why the parents would have been nervous about Euglossa.

Yet resistance to celebrating a large group of young women living together, attending university, and training for positions of leadership ran deeper than that. Traditional 19th century tomes known as the *Chbap Srei* or *Girl Law*, and *Chbap Bros* or *Boy Law*, circumscribed for generations proper gender roles in Khmer culture. The two versions (prose and poetry) of the *Chbap Srei* include mandates like moving softly at all times so as to make no sound, averting your eyes in the presence of men and boys, and remaining still while your husband beats you. And although most scholars had been under the impression that the text had fallen out of favor years ago, many of the girls still kept copies on their desks.

Regardless, the celebration was a smashing success. The girls spoke on political themes—land rights, democracy, gender equality—and served food to their parents. The Euglossa dorm founder was showered with gifts: Hand-made paper peacocks, fine scarves, small toys. Charming fathers with smooth but ragged-toothed smiles. Open laughter. Weathered mothers unwilling to display any emotion throughout the day, but who, on their way out the door, grabbed my forearm with both hands, tightly. How can that mean anything but, *Thanks*? Sosaryna's dad, a former soldier, started a political discussion with Amoun after lunch, and soon all the girls joined in. Afterwards, we sat around singing for three hours. Patriotic songs, traditional songs, happy songs.

And then, to be home before dark, families trundled back on their motorcycles and drove away home. Assured. Proud.

By nightfall, I was left in the computer room with Vannarin and Kimlong. They told me they were doing an exercise video together, but really they were watching DVDs of silly Korean boy hip-hop bands and hula-hooping. It was a far cry from the Euglossa education we had spent the day extolling, and that their parents had been presented with, but it. Was. Wonderful.

•    •    •

## Boy in the Dorm

However. During the Parents' Day celebration, I was introduced from the podium, and waggled my eyebrows in response. The girls found it amusing, and the parents, I hoped, read it as non-threatening. One mother, however, made a comment I could not understand. I assumed it was some sort of joke. But to her, and to the girls, it wasn't. Weeks later I was told sheepishly that one of the parents had taken issue with me, with my appearance. I had short hair, and the mom in question had interrupted the ceremony to ask when they started letting boys come stay at the dorm.

I am not concerned about my gender presentation, but being called a boy when you are a girl, in Cambodia, is supposed to be mean.

•    •    •

## The Real Thing is Very True

Kimlong and I sat together on the floor next to my tiny bunk bed looking at pictures on my computer. Pictures from Cheung Eck. She did not want to see pictures of my house—she didn't register this as a livable space, with so many books (the national library had been turned into stables under the Khmer Rouge, and had only recently rebuilt its a collection of books), a couch ("What happens when it rains?" another girl had asked when she saw it), and a bedroom I shared with no one. She wanted to see only pictures of Cambodia, and have me tell her what I know about her country. When we came upon the pictures I had taken at Cheung Eck, we had a talk about them.

"It is so sad." She said. "Because it have a lot of skulls. It's quiet and scary."

"Have you heard about it before?" I asked.

"I hear about it from you. I'm so surprised with everything in there," she said. Kimlong's demeanor was somber. "The bones and everything. I never believe that it happened. That it can happen. The real thing is very true. I read a little about the history in Pol Pot regime. They want to change this country different, agricultural. This is the important thing in Pol Pot regime. Especially they want to kill the Cambodian people. Sometimes they make a woman get married with a different man."

Kimlong was studying to be a lawyer and had access to history books and texts most didn't. The Khmer Rouge had abolished laws—so many laws. And rights. Marriages, yes. To re-order society. Forced marriages were common, but divorce even thirty years later was rare. Many forced marriages continued. Year Zero was much more than a propagandistic catch phrase. It was the moment everyone started anew, whether or not they wanted to.

"Does it make you angry?" I asked her.

"Yeah." She said. "I'm not just angry in this day. I'm angry a long time ago. I'm still angry right now." She spoke in sweet voice. All the girls did. A lilting, infantilized, high-pitched tone considered proper and ladylike, even behind closed doors. Even with other women. But now her sweet voice cracked with rage.

The image in front of us showed a bone poking out of the ground. It was unexpected and disgusting, and Kimlong flashed raw fury. For just a second. Then she told me a story.

"Do you know," she asked, "At my high school, we have a lot like this? We have a lot of people that are killed there. When I was young I was just small. My neighbor and I, we always go to my high school and we dig in the ground and we take a lot of bones. We take it to my parents. But my parents always blame me. 'Why you take it? Do not take any.' Very angry. They were angry and yell to me. But they do not explain. I don't know. I wanted to see it. In Prey Veng, in my province, have a lot of place that Pol Pot regime take people to kill people. Where they take the children to hit with the tree."

The Prey Veng province, in the Southeast of the country, was hit especially hard in the America bombings, before the Khmer Rouge. People there, it is said, were angry.

"What was it like to grow up there? It sounds like it would be sad and difficult," I wanted to know.

"It was so quiet and have a lot of birds and wind blow. But we scare." She said. "I am feel unhappy"—*Un. Hap. Py.*—"when I see this." She pointed to another image, of an open field, a mass grave not yet excavated. "And so sad and so sorry. At everything that's happened.

"This is destroy our country and our people. Not grow. Still make it down and down. And this regime gone out now, but our country still poor. This regime is the *Sahow*—like destroy? But big destroy.

"If I meet a Khmer Rouge I want to hit him, knock him. Everything that I can do." She said. "But I don't know their heart. What their heart build from? If they do this action with other people, I don't mind. But how they do this to Cambodia?"

3

## An Education

•　　•　　•

### Lili Tells Me Something

I had heard the story twice already, but I was obviously still missing the point, because Lili started in, again, about her teacher. She's young, she's beautiful, she's kind. Yes. She helped Lili to study. Yes. She let Lili sit in front of the classroom. Yes. She gave Lili extra assignments. My brain tried to fit this in: Was Cambodian gratefulness here just on overdrive? Plenty of public school teachers in the U.S.— underpaid, as they must be here, too—perform such heroic acts. They are dedicated, and unusual, sure. But they are also simply good at their jobs.

"Anne." Lili said. Her intensity, the import of her message, packed into this one word, my name. A few days ago, there had been a poisonous frog in the bathroom. Poisonous, but cute. I am a stupid American, and I didn't know it was poisonous, was only excited about the cuteness. I dragged Lili in to see it and she adopted the same tone then that she took with me now.

"Anne." She had said that day, very grave. She held my arm tightly and looked pointedly at the frog. "If he spit on you, you for sure will have a problem."

Lili's eyes, when talking about her teacher, had the same piercing quality. "Anne." She said. "My teacher, she does not ask for thanks you money."

•　　•　　•

### Teaching in Cambodia

In Cambodia, education is conducted via recitation and rote memorization, which makes the students obedient and attentive, but also makes things like providing a space for creative expression essentially impossible.

I had committed to teaching a self-publishing class three times per week, during which we would explore the basics of zine construction, distribution, personal expression, graphic design, illustration, and written English. I planned to bring in a few guest speakers to explain what self-publishing is and how it operates, as well as the history of related forms like comics and newspapers in Cambodia. So that we would have content to work with, I had decided to hold Friday afternoon writing seminars. In my writing class, I would announce, we are just going to write.

"Write what?" They would ask.

"Anything you want."

"About what?" They would ask.

And after a few more minutes of this we would come up with a topic, which, if I was not careful, would be the first thing that came out of my mouth, unanimously agreed to, as if I had decreed it. "Let's write about a happy time with our family," we agreed once. "Let's write how it will be for us in ten years," or "Let's write every single thing we did since we woke up." Anything to get them to imbue language with a sense of urgency, purposefulness. To expound on topics that had not first been dictated—not by me, not by teachers, not by their government. To consider anything in their paths worthy of engagement. This was meant to be exploratory, participatory, and inherently critical. It didn't always work.

Like one day I was running late for class, and Chandara was the only one who showed up. "Let's have a discussion," I said. "About the Pol Pot years."

I'd been nervous to get into the Khmer Rouge regime with these charming girls, who, truth be told, deserved nothing less than serene happiness for every moment of their lives. They are each as wonderful as Chandara; each with long, dark hair and wild laughter and smart, smart, smart. My nervousness in bringing up the topic felt appropriate, befitting a single American woman living at the whim and mercy of thirty-two spazzy Cambodian girls who, when they want to, and despite their intellectual capabilities, can get together in a mass to cry over sappy movies. Bringing up a significant and likely painful matter in their recent history and as an outsider seemed a bit group therapy if you know what I mean, if not also imperialist and maybe a little unfair. Not to mention how strange it is to barge into such an environment with an assumed sympathy, demanding to understand the suffering of others but still wanting to hear details of it.

Still, raw curiosity about survival during tremendous strife is undeniable. Particularly when most aspects of this recent past are obfuscated and undiscussed. And hidden communication happens to be your area of interest. After all, I had come here to help these girls document the unacknowledged. But I always remained skeptical my own motives: I love horror movies. Their parents lived through worse.

So until that day I had been cautious and patient, waiting for a natural opportunity to ask questions, an event on which to hinge a discussion. Like when Kimlong stumbled across my photographs. Like when Ms. Channy wanted to tell me her life story. I can also admit now that my patience masked a great fear. I did not want to hear details about the emotional pain of others. Let me be clear: I want to know how living in the aftermath of mass killing affects these young women, but I do not want to feel it for myself.

But Chandara did not know Cheung Eck. It would make sense that she had never been there; it's a little far away and these girls have no expendable income with which to venture into the world. The ten dollars I spent on a tuk-tuk was a third of the average Cambodian's monthly income, and two thirds of the girls' $15 monthly dorm allowance. Plus, with classes seven days per week—so excited were they by the opportunity to study, many pursue concurrent degrees at separate universities—who had time for a field trip? It would also make sense if Chandara had not wanted to go; many of the girls who knew what it was do not want to go to the former Khmer Rouge torture chamber or prison S-21, now called Tuol Sleng, where 12,000 people were estimated to have died, that sat less than a mile away from the dorm. And why would they? It is a horrible place.

But to never have heard of Cheung Eck—a curious and intelligent Cambodian who lives nine kilometers away! I was baffled. "What do you know about the Pol Pot years?" I asked Chandara.

And she freely explained, "Not very much. Our teachers do not tell us. It is hard to find out."

"I can tell you what I know," I offered.

"Yes." She said.

I began to explain what the Killing Fields were, and what it looks like at Cheung Eck; what happened there, and how you could tell. "It is small," I said, "and dusty. Nearby there are houses, there is a school. If you think about it being a field, far removed from anything, you are wrong. It is nearby other things.

"The Khmer Rouge needed a place to bring people, to kill them. So they brought people, at first about thirty per day, by truck. They waited until night, then at night they turned on loud music and killed people. They hung a speaker in a tree. Then they would bury them in giant pits, but soon they sent more and more people to be killed, sometimes 300 people per day, and they were not careful anymore. They did not always kill them at first. And so when they buried the bodies in giant pits, they poured a poison, a lye, over them. In case they'd survived. That would be bad. The lye also helped keep the smell down, but between it and the radio, I don't know if they could have covered up what they were doing. I bet everyone knew. But in Cambodia, you don't always say.

"Now, when you are there," I told Chandara, "you can see the giant pits, you can see the tree that held the speaker, you can see the field, you can see the neighbors.

"When you walk along the paths to the burial sites, to the baby tree where the young and light were killed by smashing, clothes are kicked up, unburied by your feet. Bones. There is a giant Stupa, skulls of people killed there. Giant." I told her we could look at pictures if she wanted to. She didn't want to.

"How did you hear about it?" Chandara asked.

"It is famous," I said. "All over the world. It is rare to have something so bad happen, so people talk about it—want to know about it. They teach it in schools now. Not when I was growing up, because it was still going on then and no one knew, but now."

"But why, in Cambodia, do we not know this, and in United States, you do?" She looked at me, exasperated.

That was what I had wanted *her* to tell *me*. Distress was evident in her wide eyes. I did not know how to answer, so I explained, "In the United States, there are parts of history we do not talk about either. We do not discuss the American Indians, for example—that the U.S. government killed in very great numbers because they wanted their land, because that makes the government look bad. We do not discuss about when big corporations in the United States make mistakes with medicines or foods that poison people. We do not discuss about when we go to war, how many people we killed. We only talk about how many Americans died, how sad it is for us, what we are losing." I explained. "The government does not like to acknowledge things that make it look bad. Like when you meet a new friend, you do not say, 'sometimes I am mean.'"

But I did not explain: In the United States, we do not learn that the government bombed Cambodia for many years, in secret, and that made it easier for Pol Pot to take control. We do not learn that when the Khmer Rouge came into Phnom Penh in 1975, declared Year Zero and pushed all the residents out of their homes into forced labor in the countryside, that they were telling people that the Americans were going to bomb again, that they needed to leave to the city to protect themselves and their families. We do not learn that Cambodia had every reason to believe that was true. We do not learn that when the Khmer Rouge forced city dwellers out into the countryside, killing people sometimes by simply letting them wander around in the forests until they stepped on landmines, that those landmines were not always planted by the Khmer Rouge. Many of them were American. Many of them still are.

In America, we do not learn of our own contributions to the Pol Pot years. Even though I was beginning to learn them, I did not tell Chandara. Because when you meet a new friend, you do not say, *sometimes I am mean.*

"Do you think it is good?" Chandara asked.

"No." I said. "I think it is wrong." I hesitated. "But I think it is understandable."

Dina Sun had joined us by then, her tallness and her sadness, and Amara, with the name of a fairy tale princess. Dina Sun was frustrated, too, by the difficulty of gaining information about a recent event in their country's history. Her parents had told her in great detail about life under the Khmer Rouge, her neighbors too. It was hard: Rice porridge, labor from 3 a.m. to 10 p.m. every day, then extra work. Many died. A neighboring village housed another Killing Field, a house that in the 1980s was stacked with bones that had dug themselves up, so near the surface were they. The house remained, a display with a stack of bones, for many years. Then, when people no longer wanted to be reminded, they took it down. There was a stark and impersonal memorial there now, easier to live with than sheer evidence.

So Dina Sun knew, which made her unusual. She knew facts about what had happened under Pol Pot and she was angry, which also made her unusual. To know enough to feel rage was rare in Cambodia. Rare and unwelcome. The girls here, they are supposed to be sweet, and shy, and soft-voiced. Her friends, they do not know. Her schoolmates now, they do not understand. She found this as confusing as I did.

"If they do not teach it in school, and the elders do not want to talk about it, how will we know?" Dina Sun asked.

I tried to explain then about how media is supposed to operate in a democracy. In the United States, I told the group, this is why we are supposed to have freedom of speech, to have media that is independent of the government and businesses. Because if they do not teach something in school, and people do not want to talk about it, there should still be a way to find out. There should be an accurate reflection of history. In case.

"In the United States," I said, "when the government does not want to explain about the American Indians, or the corporations, writers and artists and other people come in and learn, and then they write about it and make it so others can read about it. That way even if they don't teach what happened in school, you can go to the library, you can go to the internet, you can go to an afterschool program, you can go to your neighbor's house. And maybe they have a book, or a piece of art, or a movie, or a magazine that talks about the thing you want to know about, that talks about the thing you can't get anyone to tell you," I said.

"Like how we are doing with our zines." We had just made our first batch of small, self-published booklets that week, trundled them off to the neighborhood copyshop (branded with a hand-painted and hilarious sign that read "Minotal"), and brought them to the bookstore to distribute. Practice for later, when we really had something to say.

"Now you know how to make media that is outside of government control, that isn't associated with a business." I said. "If you want to, you can start to change what people know."

•       •       •

*Learning Khmer*

*A Ni Die.* This is an arm.

*Sok So Bie.* How are you?

*Phkou.* Flower.

*Chum Reap Leal.* Goodbye, it was nice to meet you.

*Sompto.* Sorry.

*Tu Rup Sop Die.* Mobile telephone.

*Aw Kun.* Thanks.

*Kroma.* Scarf.

*Jach.* Banana.

*High Five.* Same in both languages.

*Waihnta.* Glasses.

*Jot.* Grody.

*Porm.* Apple.

*Groch.* Orange.

*Sork.* Hair.

I am practically fluent.

. . .

*Personal Question*

Narin wondered if she could ask me a personal question.

"OK," I said. I thought she was going to ask something about underwear. I am not always fond of it, when it is hot. I had learned this in Nicaragua, where underpants-wearing and yeast infections have a high correlation. Not for me, of course—I lucked out and got cholera, which nearly killed me and sent me home before other ailments could befall me—but for most people. Also, I lived with three girls in a room that was maybe ten feet square. They were curious about things, but they did not always ask. Underwear might be one of the things.

Ah, but she asked what I wanted to do when I grew up.

"I am grown up," I said. I was 37. I was exactly twice her age. "This is what I do. I go places and I learn and I teach things to people and then I write about them. Sometimes I do not get paid for this, but it is what I do."

We were making zines. We were in day three of the zine-making project and I was sort of dreading it. I did not think they were catching on. I think they enjoyed it, sure, but did not believe it was important. The week before I had tried to alleviate my growing concern by putting it in context, by comparing our zines to the *Cambodia Daily*, to some of the comics I'd brought with me from Chicago to show them, media projects that just take a few people to put together.

And the girls saw that you can learn from all of them, and that they all take talent and work. But they revere the *Cambodia Daily*, one of two English-language papers in the country, but the only one published every day. There was nothing else you can learn *as much* from. The things you learn from it were *more important.* They had a class on it in the dorm, a new one on each day's paper, so refuting its significance was tantamount to girl treason at Euglossa. No girls, ever, they felt, could do anything as important as the *Cambodia Daily*. So Vannarin—she used the nickname Narin, among friends—said, "You have a lot of freedom."

"Sort of," I said. Anything probably looks like freedom to a girl who's been told she must be married by 24. "But I have a lot of responsibility, too," I told her. "It is hard work. Do you know how you are supposed to have freedom of speech here in Cambodia? But you do not, really? Making zines with you is a way of showing you how to have some of that anyway. In a safe way."

"But it is not safe," she said. "In the school, sometimes the teacher, he cannot say the truth. Like when we talk about the corruption, or the past. Angkor Wat or the Pol Pot period. Because the students, we don't know their parents. Who are they?"

"Wait," I said. "Your teacher cannot teach because of the students?" The Khmer Rouge years had been skipped over in history texts, I knew, but that seemed to be a different issue.

"Yes. You do not know what their parents will say. You do not know what they will do. If you want to know the real history of Cambodia, you learn by yourself. There are books."

"Books." I said. We went on like this for some time. I clarified, I asked questions. It was unclear to me what the parents would do, or the students. Or why each should be feared. It did not get much clearer, because talking about the causes of fear can be very difficult. Pinning root concerns down to definable, separate actions—this is not always possible.

"People get hurt," she said earnestly. And I know this was true, but it was true everywhere. And anyway we were in class, so I was looking for an angle, a way to explain to her the tool that I was hoping to provide her.

"Well, I said, if you do not want to speak about things, you can always write them down. Look, here is a zine. You can put all the information you want in it and give it to people or leave it places for them to find."

And she said, "But do you have to put your name on it?"

"No," I explained. "You do not. If you are scared to put your name on it, you do not have to. But it might be important for people to hear your ideas. Maybe they will have some of their own to share."

"Like writing to the government," she said. "You can write them a letter and tell them to change something."

"Yes," I said, "but that does not always work."

"Sometimes they think, 'We are the government! We know better.'" Narin agreed.

"Yes," I nodded. "But sometimes if you have enough people who have the same ideas, it can be as big as the government. The government will want to listen."

"Ah," Narin said. "Many voices unified can be stronger."

"Yes," I said.

"And what I do is, I help unify voices." I held up one of the zines. "That is my job."

•     •     •

*Later That Afternoon*

Then I met with a woman whose name I cannot give you.

I wanted to ask her about corruption in the government, about some of the things that Narin had told me.

"Teachers," I asked her, "they cannot teach because they fear the students?"

"Yes," she agreed. "They fear that they will go back to their parents and repeat what they learned in school and the parents will make repercussions."

When you became accustomed to a student vocabulary as filtered through the Khmer accent, it was surprising to hear the word, repercussions.

"For example, corruption." She said. "If the teacher teaches honestly about government corruption, and the student goes home to talk to the parents, and the parents work for the government, the parents might ask, 'Who is this teacher?' And they may be threatened. People disappear."

In my mind, and from what Narin had told me, this still seemed an unreasonable fear.

"What are the chances that a teacher will teach about corruption, and then a student in the class would be living in the household of a corrupt government employee?" Slim, I deduced silently. I was assuming that not every single government employee could possibly be corrupt. I told my friend this.

"It is not always the government employee," she said patiently. "Sometimes it is the wife, the children. If you want a new job, for example, you do not go to your boss. You go to bring $10,000 to his wife, and you say, 'I would like a new job.' So at night, she will lobby for you. She will say to you, 'I will get you this job and if you do not get it, I will return this money.' The children too. Much powerful is wife."

"So can you give me an idea of how rampant corruption is," I asked. "Is it many people, some people? I do not understand."

"All the people." She said. "All the people. I quit my job because of the corruption. I used to work with the government. Once, I was invited, let's say, to go to Paris for a conference, and I had to go to apply for my visa. And so you go to the first office. He says, 'OK, I will process your application. Ten dollars.' But he is a government employee. He is supposed to process the applications. And every government staff receives a salary, right? And he is only the *first one* who must approve the application. Above him is," and she stacks her hands together, many times on top of each other. Maybe eight times.

"Above him are others." She said. "So I tell him, 'I do not have ten dollars. I have not even been approved to go to Paris yet. If I am approved, maybe I will give you ten dollars. But I need to be approved.' 'Oh,' he tells me. And leaves the application on his desk for many weeks.

"While," she said, "he has lunch, he plays golf." Weeks later she goes back. "'My application?' I ask. 'Ten dollars,' he says."

Her salary at the time was fifteen dollars, she told me. Per month.

"'When you pay me ten dollars, I will process your application.' he says." The conference in Paris is calling in the meantime, too: *When are you arriving? Why has your paperwork not been processed yet?*

But she could not explain why. It was simply too ridiculous. Later, she had a job with a non-governmental organization where she tracked weapons proliferation. The government, she said, did not update their records. They released information about weapons that was untrue. So she gave interviews with the press about this issue, and she talked about it publicly. It was her job. And she began to receive phone calls every couple of months.

"From: No number," she said, surprised. "My friends, my husband, they all have numbers that appear. But there was no number. A ghost!"

And the ghost said to her, "Do not do any more interviews. There could be an accident."

"Were you scared?" I asked her.

"No," she said. "I left my job. And you are saying to yourself, why leave your job if you are not scared?"

"No," I told her seriously, shaking my head. "I'm not. That's ridiculous. I would be sick of it. I would not want to be around it anymore."

"Exactly," she said. There was a pause. But she had more to say. "My husband, he would not want me to tell you this." She breathed. "He wanted to be a freelance contractor, but he worked for the government. So he applied to be a freelance contractor, because the salary is very good—$1,200 per month. But to be a freelance contractor, you can't work for the government. So he went to his boss and said, 'I would like to be a freelance contractor, but I have to quit my job here.' 'No you don't,' his boss said. 'You can stay working here, and you can get the freelance contracting job, but you must give me all your government salary and half the freelance contracting salary. And if you do not, you will not pass the interview.'"

She looked at me. "He was the one giving the interview," she said.

"So I told my husband, 'Look in your heart. Do you want the experience, or do you want the salary?' And he thought about it and decided he wanted the experience. So he went to his boss and said, 'If I pass the interview and am offered the job, I will give you this.' And seven people passed the interview, but only my husband was offered the job. And so now, every month, he goes and gets his salary, takes half of it out of the bank, gives it to his boss. He works eight or more hours every day, and then he comes home at night and works more, sometimes until one in the morning."

It may help you to understand why this was crazy in Cambodia to realize that people got up at 5.

"So let me get this straight," I asked her. "It seems like I must have missed something. Your husband, he works two full time jobs?"

"Yes."

"And he takes home half the salary from only one of the jobs?"

"Yes." She said. She was almost laughing. "It is funny. It is also sad."

"He takes home $600 per month?"

"Yes." She said.

"That is ridiculous."

"Yes." She said. "And that is not all. When new babies are born, they receive a stipend from the government. Two thousand riel per month." Approximately $.50, and yes, you read that right. When her new baby was born, her husband went to fill out the birth certificate, and they said, *you will not receive your stipend for the first year, because we will keep it. After that, you will receive your stipend.*

"Oh." I was catching a glimmer of something. A cycle that starts at birth. A thing that seems natural because so common. A banal evil. "What, then, is *thanks you* money?" I inquired. I used Lili's phrase, word for word, syllable for syllable.

My friend said, "The teacher, she or he is supposed to get paid by the government—$30, $35. But they do not always pay. Sometimes it is late.

Sometimes it does not arrive at all. So the teacher must ask the students for money—to live, you see. If you do not pay you must sit"—and she waved her arm across the room—"Far. Many student in classroom. Fifty, more. You cannot hear far.

"If you do not pay thanks you money," my friend explained, "you do not learn."

"And that's OK," I stated, mimicking her flat tone, her sense of finality. "There is nothing you can do."

She remained silent. She was waiting for me to finish, willing me to stop talking so the truth of what I was repeating back to her could sink in.

When it did, I asked, "How come you don't just walk around punching people? All day long?"

"My husband, he is calmer than I am." She said. "We have bad government now, but next year is an election year. We hope. We hope it will change. My husband is calm, all the time, except when he drives."

4

## Urban Planning

•    •    •

### It Does Happen

In Phnom Penh many of the drivers on the road had just arrived from the provinces where there are few, if any, rules of the road besides honking at chickens. They went fast and rarely bumped into things as there were fewer of them there. They did not need maps, because in the provinces there was a main road and the road they lived on and then if you were really in the thick of it, another road someone else they probably knew lived on.

So you travelled by remote sensing, by landmark, by the vague gnaw in your gut that when you saw the place you were supposed to be you would recognize it and so it was hopefully on the road on which you happened to be driving, fast, without bumping into things or maybe bumping into them sometimes but hopefully not but it does happen.

Driving in Phnom Penh was like any gathering where several hundred people that felt this way came together, say at a convention where they discuss these issues, or like at a party for *hooray we drive crazy*, or maybe even, for example, on a road together driving fast motos.

You cannot know what it was like unless you imagine a churning pool at the base of a large waterfall made of sharp metal and tender exposed skin, or that you had been dropped into a videogame where all of the characters have guns and are in it for themselves, and although you can see it all, and know the score, you don't know which character you are playing. Nothing responds to your commands, no one acknowledges you; no one acknowledges anything. They are just going where they want. Just try to imagine this for a minute, aloof from the action that you can see unfolding and then as you are imagining it realize that even in your imagination, your imagined self is pulling back, is cautious, doesn't want to get too close.

And sometimes there were traffic lights. Why would you put a traffic light in a churning pool or a videogame? There is no way it will help. But there were four traffic lights at each of the five main intersections in Phnom Penh.

The rules for these were supposed to be the same: Stop on red, go on green, say that you slow down on amber but actually speed up to avoid sitting there, thinking, I could have made it.

But we learn these rules in traffic school in the U.S., or when we apply for our driver's licenses. Both were rare here. Cambodia remains an oral culture so rules spread by rumor, or watching. So at every traffic light, the drivers watched each other. He is stopping, I will stop. All sides, stopped at the same time sometimes. Or maybe one would go, and then it all changed.

One day I had a moto accident. I was waiting at a traffic light, abiding the laws I was familiar with, of not going on red, when a woman on a bike with two toddlers—one in front and one behind—seemingly wanted to drive through me, to just take a shortcut right, I don't know, over the top of me or ghost-like disappear into the invisible portal I didn't know about on my left and show up a moment later to my right. I was a few yards back from the intersection, jammed sardine-style into the mouth of the road, and she was exactly perpendicular to me. I don't know why. To achieve her goal, she drove headlong toward me, just tried to barrel right through, one kid in front and one behind. On a bike. Then she tipped over.

The kids didn't fall off or anything; I didn't even tip over. But still. You just can't do that. Drive through a person like that.

Add to all this the overburdening of some motos with hundreds of chickens, entire families, mattresses, stacks of caged pigs; a disinterest in helmets; and the road rage that, at least in nearby Vietnam, where streets are more congested but laws adhered to, kills some 1,200 motorists per month, and which here in Phnom Penh allowed occasional accidents to be followed up by bloody, to-the-death fistfights, which would up the mortality rate attributable to road rage if the government didn't have a vested interest in not tallying these numbers. Well. Combined, it was quite something.

●     ●     ●

## Date With a Fixer

I could not refuse the offer to exchange phone numbers with someone whose job it was to get others out of trouble via extralegal means.

After all, when I couldn't find a moto one night, he had gallantly borrowed his brother's and driven me home—not for money, as a favor, and even before that I'd been told: "That guy, he gets stuff done. He knows everyone." Which is not, normally, something that impresses me. But his job title did: Fixer. He could turn a visa around in a few hours, score you tickets to anything in town, spring you from the clink on a moment's notice, even if you were American. Even if your imprisonment was justified. Um, also: He was young, scrappy. Clearly understood power dynamics in a way most people can't. Clever. Or rather, cute.

So, OK, he dropped me at home once and then offered to *missed call to me*, which is where I tell him my phone number and he calls it and I don't answer but I do have his number now. Most Cambodians have cell phones, but many cannot afford to purchase the minutes necessary to speak on them, so text-messaging and even missed-calling become communication mediums of their own. *The person with this number is thinking of you*, it means sometimes. Or, *the person with this number is running late*. Or, *the person with this number would like you to call them*.

The fixer spent a lot of time with foreigners. It seemed natural to me that he would want to hang out. Sometimes people are just more comfortable with others of dissimilar backgrounds. A reasonable cross-cultural friendship could result from this missed-call-to-me thing, I rationalized.

But he was definitely not in this for the hang-out time, as he took me to the nicest restaurant in town. Because he's a landowner, I didn't feel the slightest bit weird about that, economically speaking, although for any other Cambodian I knew, I would have offered to pay.

To be honest, I'm not sure I was really in it for hang-out time, either: I wanted to know what a fixer does all day. I wanted to know what a fixer's life is like. I wanted to know how a fixer spends his evenings. Apparently they spend them having explicit sexualized conversations with girls, because our food had not arrived before he was telling me how tired he was of Khmer prostitutes and how he much preferred foreign girlfriends.

It was a ham-fisted invitation and, although I am daft, it did not go unnoticed by me. But I was *definitely* not in this for the sexual experimentation. And most certainly not interested in a relationship. Prostitutes aside, he claimed to be. Interested in a relationship. For the most part. He slipped up a few times and mentioned having a girlfriend, although he would then try to explain that actually, she got married two years ago and now he was available. And by now he meant, now. Had I finished my dinner?

I had not. It had just arrived at the table. I initiated conversation. What province was he from? When had he come to the city? Among the information I gleaned from him: He moved to the city alone at 13 to go to high school. He comes from the classic broken home, which in Khmenglish is when one's husband or father *gets a new wife*. A new wife does not usually indicate a legal remarriage, and doesn't always entail a divorce from the old wife. Sometimes this happens quite suddenly. Sometimes the old wife does not know.

The fixer had traveled some, was a mover and a shaker, had been to Australia, was 26. Also: Liked to sleep with English girls, was into tongue, preferred to spend his free time watching TV or getting a blow job. Really liked romance.

"Romance," I repeated. I tilted my head to the side. I couldn't place the word.

"Romance," he said again. As if it were a common concept. He elaborated. First he described it as being the opposite of what girls in bars want—prostitutes. So, sex? Money? To survive in a culture hostile to women's rights? To feed their kids? I didn't know what girls in bars in Cambodia wanted, since I had not visited a bar. I lived in a dorm. My friends were 17. Most of them had never seen a beer. A beer? When I go to a bar, I want a beer. I was pretty sure *romance* did not mean the opposite of *beer*.

"Like on a couch," he said. And repeated the word for emphasis: "Romance." The way he drew it out I finally understood it to mean: Mutual physical pleasure.

"And what about you? What do you like?" He asked me as we finished our meal. I'd now cracked the code sufficiently to understand that a list of my favorite books was not an appropriate response. His question meant, sexually.

*What do you like, sexually?* It was the first question he'd asked me. Clearly, fixers believe a lengthy monologue is seductive.

"Oh, Christ." I breathed out through my mouth. I couldn't help it. He hadn't caught my interjections throughout his monologue, intended to convey: *This is your trip, dude.* A feminist construct snapped together in my mind like a magical self-building geodesic dome. He had advertised mutual physical pleasure, put it right out there, a perk should I choose to take him up on his offer of couch time. An add-on. A service he rendered for his own ultimate enjoyment. Neither standard nor necessary. Certainly not: What I might like was, literally, an afterthought.

"Look." I said. I settled for tact. "I'm quite a bit older than you. Romance doesn't really fit into my life right now," I told him. Not to mention that it wouldn't fit in before curfew, which was in about 20 minutes.

"No, I am 26," he said. "You are 16, 17." He said it slowly, patiently: Because I did not understand. I was a silly girl.

I laughed out loud. "No, I'm 37," I said. I told you I looked young.

"You—what? No." He was baffled. However, he was in no way put off.

Which, oh man. It is one thing to be in an organic conversation and caught up in emotional potential and mystery and discovery and excitement about someone and it is mutual in a genuine way. But it is totally another when you aren't caught up in anything. When there is nothing organic going on except that the man that you are with, he apparently feels comfortable talking at length about his physical interests, and expects you to feel just as enthusiastic about them. Your own interests, your own physical demands, your own expressions thereof, these are irrelevant. These are not present. These do not matter. You are a girl. This was Cambodia.

But he was a very sweet boy, and something of a dangerous one, so in further pursuit of tactful disentanglement I feigned sudden exhaustion.

He pouted. Why, I don't know. He hadn't even actually been spurned—I'd been excessively careful about that. Perhaps my total disinterest was clear, although I doubt it: He continued with the hypersexual chit chat, describing his penis, displaying his tongue, making lewd hand gestures. My heart went out to the prostitutes who had worked with him in the past. This was boring.

A class act in the end, or more likely sure I would change my mind *en route*, he did drive me home. Without me asking him to, but because it was only proper, he left me about ten meters away from my doorstop so I wouldn't have to deal with the prying eyes of the neighbors, or the judgment of the dorm's night staff. All were likely to be in apparent agreement with the fixer, in believing that white women could only want one thing from Cambodian men.

. . .

## Commerce

The tourist guidebooks say to haggle over every U.S. dollar in the markets as if your life depended on it. But I started thinking: It's going to be much easier for me to replace that dollar than it would be for the shopkeeper in front of me. It is not worth a dollar for me to strong-arm her into lowering her prices in order to feel like I won this shopping experience. Concession and demand should not dictate how I interact with people, for one, and for two: Do I really need to feel victorious when I go shopping?

Visiting Siem Reap did not help, of course. A circus of competing Disneylands, Siem Reap is, sure, home to magnificent temples, fascinating history, vast entertainments and, unlike most of the rest of the country, modern conveniences to rival those designed for outer space. It was a more popular destination than Phnom Penh, which was described in those same tourist guidebooks as worth a day, if you have one to spare. In Siem Reap, I knew for a fact I was being taken advantage of, partly due to my gender. Most of the shopkeepers and service people I dealt with there were men, and most were charging me double or triple what I'd refuse to haggle over with women in Phnom Penh. And men—sometimes they try to pull one over on you.

But today I was back in my beloved capital city, and thankful the tourists didn't stay for long. I had an errand to run in Psar Toul Tom Pong, the Russian Market. This is the market described in the guidebooks as the one to really haggle at—where people are genuinely trying to screw you, since they stole their stuff from the Gap manufacturing plant anyway. Why that argument would fly for even half a second I couldn't quite fathom: I wholeheartedly support stealing from the Gap.

The guidebooks go on: Shopkeepers have the nerve to charge you up to two dollars for a shirt that cost them nothing! Maybe even three dollars! For something you would gladly pay thirty for at a Gap in the States. It is kind of assumed in guidebooks that you shop at Gaps in the States. Maybe you do, I don't know. I do not. But what the guidebooks don't mention is that nearly 300,000 garment workers in Cambodia earn less than half a living wage making those shirts under ever-worsening conditions. The textile industry is the nation's third largest income generator, but it's even more important than that fact alone might indicate: The salaries of garment workers support a fifth of the country, including most of the farmworkers in provinces back home. Since rice production remains the nation's second largest money-maker, neither industry could survive without the income of the garment workers. For what you might pay for a pair of Gap slacks, a garment worker supports herself and her family every month, and bolsters the only economic infrastructure Cambodia has. Far as I'm concerned, anyone smart enough to siphon a bit of profit off for themselves has earned their two dollars. Maybe even three!

Not the point, though: I was at the market to pick up gifts to send back home, and came across a cute young shopkeeper selling gorgeous scarves. I watched in a stupor as two different groups of tourists from two different regions of the world mauled her display, throwing scarves everywhere, disenchanted with this color or that fabric or unsure whether or not this one might match a particular beloved and apparently well-remembered jacket. The tourists were vomiting privilege, setting the scene for a total shopping victory. One group stormed off quickly, thoroughly dissatisfied with her shop's selection, refusing even to answer her question, "How much you pay?" before they ransacked someone else's display. The other group requested a four-dollar item for a dollar.

"Three dollars," she said. Then they walked away too.

The shopkeeper was rightfully pissed, I think; she'd been treated without a shred of human decency by two different representative groups from two different nations. On her behalf, I hated the world.

She started refolding the items, resolutely. I was watching her, sort of, but also looking at what she had for sale. I wanted to buy something. Partially out of the urge to be nice to her, and partially out of the urge to—hell, people, it's *raw silk*. What was I gonna do? She had for sale an orange scarf in raw silk, which is kind of like saying, "Hey Anne, here is everything you've ever wanted in a single item. Would you like to own it in exchange for not very much money?"

So I asked the young shopkeeper the price in Khmer, and she answered, brightly and relieved, in Khmer. Then I had to say, in English, "I'm sorry, I only understand how to ask things in Khmer. I do not understand the answers."

She laughed, and gave me a price, and I bought the item. She proceeded to fold another pretty thing that I quite liked, and I commented on it in Khmer, and she held it up to me like you would hold a pink lace dress up to a sweet but dirt-covered child, daintily and respectfully. But not too close. It was one of the scarves the tourists had earlier discarded.

"For you, two dollars," she said. And then taught me some scarf-related Khmer words. Soon we were laughing about my pronunciation, about the customers that just left, about global capitalism. It was funny sometimes.

Of course there is ego involved in haggling, in conquering, and then in owning. I understand that sometimes a person gets caught up in it and can't extract themselves. In fact, that is what ego does. But I also understand that global capitalism makes the privileged feel already like something has been taken from them, from us, and this is rarely true. When I walked away from her shop, I had received a ridiculously good price on silk goods, had laughed with her, and had learned a few new vocabulary words. What I had given up were a handful of dollars and a few moments of kindness.

I said goodbye in Khmer. As I left, she touched my arm and said, thankfully in English, "I am really glad to meet you."

•     •     •

## Marketing Genocide

One of the very weirdest things about traveling in Cambodia is that by dint of needing to survive, locals sell access to their most horrifying experiences, to any comer, and thus must find a way to present them appealingly. Walking around the central area, for example, tuk-tuk drivers kept approaching me to ask gleefully if I'd like to go see the Killing Fields! Unless they didn't speak

English, in which case they would just brightly pose, "Killing Field?" and raise an eyebrow as I walked by.

"No, thank you," I said, over and over again. *No, thank you* to the Killing Fields. The bright enthusiasm disturbs, however necessary it may prove for the country's economic development. Especially when many who live in the country we're talking about either don't know about the Khmer Rouge or would prefer not to discuss them. And what sane person *would* prefer to discuss them? The agreed-upon avoidance makes perfect emotional sense. The mass decision to skirt the topic, call that era the Pol Pot years and cast them a national tragedy, the doing of one bad man. It was better, probably, healthier than recounting specific family members lost for now inexplicable reasons or months, years of acute starvation. Violence suffered or, just as frequently, delivered.

Unless, of course, you have decided to make your living as an informal tour guide of the Killing Fields. In which case you must put on display your very worst experiences, borrowed or invented if not lived, but polished and emotionless regardless so those who are willing to pay to hear them do not go home scarred. *Caveat Emptor:* The system is flawed.

Just add it to the extensive list of understood, but rarely investigated, trauma. The stories that do get told of the Pol Pot years are short and uncomfortable, barely scratching the surface of the emotionally complex relationship the nation has with the Khmer Rouge regime.

I was introduced to such stories one night at a screening of ten short student documentaries from a local university. Each film, on the subject of the Pol Pot years, was less than five minutes long, and completed in under five weeks. Due to the subject matter and scarcity of editing facilities, students worked on them primarily during class time. Receiving permission to stay after school hours or extra funding for more equipment or lab monitors was unthinkable. The films were, therefore, rushed. To this journalist almost irresponsible: So many questions unasked, so many questionable figures unaccused, so many issues addressed only through metaphor. And still, the films were profound.

One collected interviews with local villagers about a killing field memorial in Kran Tachan. A stupa had been built, and bones, endless bones of the dead, collected. But locals wanted to dismantle it. They succinctly explained to the young filmmaker, and to us, why they would prefer to have no memorial whatsoever;

why they would prefer to move on. A cohesive argument for forgetting. In another film, a man appointed to a medicine-making position under the Khmer Rouge described his unlearned and happenstance approach to medical care under duress. Descriptions of rabbit feces, ground sticks, poisons used as medicine. Would all be funny if not true. In another, a musician told of his career as an Angkar entertainer, in the film eloquently forgetting the lyrics to the propaganda songs he had sung for troops and workers, often their only distraction from starvation. His, too.

The films were watchable, if light on facts or indictments. Sometimes humorous. Largely human, and always so respectful.

Yet, as the students described screening their first films at home, a clear consensus among the older generation emerged. Their parents—none of whom had spoken about their own experiences in the Pol Pot years, the students complained— grew silent. No praise or pride was offered their children. No acknowledgement of effort. All ten families suffered the films wordlessly, the young filmmakers described. Nine families never mentioned them again. Only one student's father queried his son later, at the dinner table. He asked why his son had spent so much time and energy and money talking about something so bad. After the sloppily doled out chunks of honesty and raw emotion we'd witnessed on video, this young filmmaker's stumbling narrative rang truer than any first-person survivor's tale. A trauma survivor does not want to discuss or watch films about trauma.

There was something to it, even from a cultural perspective. Not much can be surmised from a close study of mass killing that can't be gleaned from an afterschool special: People do great evil for very little reason. We know this instinctually, and no amount of further learning, it seems, has compelled us to find a way to stop it.

In the particular case of Cambodia, we cannot even apply the lessons of other genocides: The term refers to the deliberate execution of ethnic racial, religious, or national groups as distinct from the executioners' own. Certainly, there was a genocide in Cambodia: Cham Muslims were targeted, ethnic Vietnamese as well. Yet the majority of ethnic Khmer killed under Pol Pot were killed by other ethnic Khmer, a fact that confuses the issue both legally and domestically.

Even the outcomes of these mass killings are not subject to easy Western comprehension. Post Traumatic Stress Disorder is the name we give the experience of trauma survivors after they have left a traumatic environment. In Cambodia, however: People farmed rice in poverty before Pol Pot. Under Pol Pot, they farmed rice in poverty. And after Pol Pot, they farmed more rice in poverty. Social workers struggle to name and respond to a temporary worsening of already harsh conditions. Poverty before the Khmer Rouge was already traumatic, and hasn't ended yet.

The language of suffering offers a particular problem when codified, when commodified. Like the tuk-tuk drivers in the central area, these student films—in English—were arguably presented for an American audience. Certainly a Western one. So too are Cheung Eck and Tuoul Sleng, memorials of mass torture and killing. The language, abbreviated, describes the experience, vaguely. There is room for interpretation and ambivalence in the free market. As long as someone is buying it.

Many did. The tuk-tuk drivers who gleefully offered visits to Cheung Eck as alternatives to golf or the equally popular shooting ranger were busy enough. A young boy at the entrance to Tuoul Sleng first impressed passersby with his English and then asked them for money. His story made for brisk sales.

"How old are you?" I asked him.

"12," he said.

"Where are your parents?" Asking after families is a sign of respect. Sometimes.

"We don't have," he said, gesturing to a shorter kid a few meters away.

"Where are they?" I asked.

"Killed by Pol Pot."

He was too young for that to be true, but the woman next to me mumbled concern and handed him a dollar. He has benefited from her lack of knowledge.

It happens on a larger scale, too. A Japanese company manages Cheung Eck, and charged international visitors two dollars each. Cambodians need not pay at all, but few visited in 2007. The previous year, international visitors to the site had doubled.

The profits rolled in. It's called *development*.

5

## THE ADVANTAGE AND DISADVANTAGE OF DORM

•          •          •

*Zine*

More and more, every day, even the girls I never ever saw—the ones in pre-med, the ones with boyfriends, the ones who pretended they could not speak English at all and therefore made pretenses to avoid me even though I suspected they were just shy—dropped tiny little zines off at my desk. One-page, eight-fold-style zines. One cut, six interior pages, totally self-contained.

I had a friend translate the how-to document I made into Khmer and left it and copies of an English version throughout the dorm. Occasionally I would stumble across the young women showing each other how to fold and where to cut, and discussing what sorts of things they might put in there.

"Sister, I made this." They would say when they were done. "*Bong*, is for you."

Elaborate drawings of things they grew up with and miss: Certain kinds of rice, mostly, or houses on stilts. Dina Sun had been fond of drawing as a child and was showered with art awards. But when she was old enough, her mother forbade her from drawing, unless with a stick in the dirt. Art was not considered productive, not entrepreneurial enough. Her zine was filled with elaborate landscapes. Every color we had access to. We went all out on the photocopies, too, which required a field trip to a copyshop that was not in someone's living room, did not make the awkwardly spelled Minotal copies. A copyshop with more than one machine, and several stacks of paper. Full color. As many as we could afford, every week.

Other Khmer young lady zinesters concentrated on domestic topics: Baby brothers, people who wear the checked scarf Kroma for entire outfits, the water buffalo they left behind. With small English explanations for their international readers: *This a popular house style in Cambodia*, one might say. *This is the best game we play.*

But to me they explain, "There is my mom. She is making rice. I used to climb this tree. I helped plant that field. I was only six, but my brother let me come with. He said, 'If you come with, you have to carry the water.' And even though the water jug was as heavy as I was, I carried it because I was happy to be with my brother." The intricacies were lost in the translation to the page.

Our zines were always in English, one concession to the concerns that the kind of democracy we might be practicing didn't jive with the ruling party's. I'm not sure now we were ever in danger, so unthinkable was it that young women might attempt even a small disobedience in Cambodian culture.

"Zine," The Euglossa girls said to me confidently. To them it was another vocabulary word, a totally regular concept that, now, 50% of the Americans they had ever lived with make on a regular basis.

"No," I told them when they would hand me a new zine. "This is not for me. I will take it, and I will make copies of it, but I want you to figure out who you want to read it. You decide who you want to share this with."

Well, everyone, of course. They wanted everyone to know about their brother and the water buffalo and the rice fields. Houses on stilts so common there, games we've never imagined playing. So I made copies, and sent them out in the mail, and then every Friday I went to the bookstore to drop off another batch. By the next Friday they would be gone, and someone would have asked about them at the cafe. And then the next Friday the people at the gallery were jealous and wanted us to distribute them there, too.

A further protection: I only distributed the zines in English-language locales, spaces mostly for tourists. Until I started getting emails. *Can you bring them to us here? And here?* "I hear you are the one who make the zine," One email began. "We are desperate for zine."

A particularly hectic Friday I had drop points all over the city, hundreds of zines, delivered on my little moto. By the time I got back, there was a note from the bookstore, the first of my drop points.

"We do not have any more zine," it said.

•        •        •

## The Craft Movement

As I was washing my clothes one afternoon, I got to thinking: I know I am supposed to be all DIY and shit, but this washing-my-own-clothes-by-hand business is totally ridiculous.

Remember, *Unmarketable* had just come out, and almost daily a new reporter or reviewer or fan would hold me up in some public forum as a purist, a person concerned wholly and exclusively with integrity and authenticity—with acknowledging the means of production for all goods and services used, all the time. It is true that this is important. It might even have explained why I went to Cambodia in the first place. I have always been attracted to poverty and ingenuity, to the use of intellectual resources to create physical ones. These are uncomplicated and eminently transferable skills and I admired them. As I had limited language abilities in Southeast Asia, life stayed very simple for me: The man pointing the gun at you was bad. The woman handing you food and stroking your knee was good. People's desires seemed straightforward: Family, a safe home, enough food. Not too terribly much else. Those who grow their own rice are safest, more likely to survive. There are more of them who do this than not. My role in the world felt well-defined.

It was a situation unlike any in the culture I'd been immersed in—Western culture. American mass culture had gotten so far away from prizing personal ingenuity that mainstream media acknowledgement, in the form of endless features on the so-called DIY movement, was required to bring back a sense that individuals could have influence on their own surroundings. A Martha Stewart show. A magazine about dumpster diving. Crafting, repurposing, recycling—whatever you call it, it was rarely presented as a means of going about a life. It was an aesthetic. You subscribed to the magazine, bought the tools, watched the show. You did not turn your television on its back, smash the screen, and use it as a planter. The website Etsy took off, craft fairs, boutique shops. You could buy anything you wanted from locally made craftspeople instead of big-box stores. The DIY movement was primarily a way to accessorize, a brand new way to consume.

Yet for me, DIY had always been action-oriented, an approach, something that must be taught and fostered and adhered to. An ethic. Sure, buying direct from makers rejects shopping-mall consumerism. But it still supports consumerism—even localizing it within those who want to consider themselves anti-capitalist.

Craftivists. Many of whom see DIY as an ethic applicable to only their mode of producing their products, and not as a way of shifting the entire system of production. In my view, *DIY* has always meant that whatever skills I have accrued, once mastered, should be passed along for free to those who could make use of them. It's this difference in approach that keeps me from giving weight to the phrase *DIY movement*: A movement is political. Not entrepreneurial.

So what I was thinking, somewhere along my third hour of scrubbing my own filth from my own underpants using a soap designed for machines I feared I might never lay eyes on again but that was the only thing available for the task as it was widely assumed to be *effing insane* to wash clothes by hand in this day and age, is that what seems to be prized by the crafting community in the States is an unmediated marketplace. A marketplace not unlike the Central Market here in Phnom Penh, where the women who make the stuff are there selling it and you go and talk to them and develop a relationship with them and you purchase stuff from them regularly. Like a toilet brush. Except: Idealized.

Central Market itself was a messy, smelly, loud place. It was also confusing, and you could really only find the right thing by stumbling upon it or asking someone about it. It was not created with a pleasant cunsumer experience in mind. Let's face it, there's a reason why people invented stores: Because sometimes you do not need to talk about toilet brushes with anyone. Certainly, you do not need to form a lasting bond with the person who sells them to you.

So it was hard for me to envision shopping of the past as a friendly, enthusiastic endeavor where human relationships played a fundamental and essential element in consumer needs, as the in-vogue DIY movement called upon me to do. And it struck me as entirely nonsensical to pretend the internet could be an easy, accessible, and cheap way to reintegrate an open, egalitarian marketplace into modern Western society. *Fuck you, DIY movement*, I thought more than once. *I don't see you out here doing your own goddamn laundry by hand. Or for that matter, starting the website Doing Laundry For You By Hand Dot Com.*

Yet by the time I was in my fifth hour of managing a process I devote no more than 20 minutes to at home, I realized that I felt a loss only crafters had begun to articulate. It wasn't the joy of buying my toilet brush from a favored stall in the crowded market that was a pain to get to and that smelled bad and that I wished most of the time I didn't have to go to. It absolutely wasn't that

I had no option but to hand wash my clothes, which tired and hurt and took time and was something that technology did a better job at than I possibly could. It wasn't moreover that the entire structure of a life changes when you must perform these activities in the course of a week; that your productivity is necessarily decreased while your time for deliberation is increased, and this did, in the end, make me feel more balanced, as much as it also sucked. It was something about innovation.

As night fell, I hung up my underpants, right there on the rack. The boys who slept on the roof opposite the Euglossa building would see them the next morning. It's not that I minded so much, or that I didn't mind. I didn't have any choice. When I described them to my roommates, dryers made them guffaw. *Machines* that make *air hot?* They would wave about themselves, the temperature perfect for drying a soaking-wet towel within an hour. Then they would look at me as if I were making things up to trick them—like, they believed, I had done with the entire concept of reality TV—and go back to work. The phrase *airing one's dirty laundry in public* loses meaning when it is the only manner in which one's laundry can be aired.

What I felt most strongly in that moment was that American culture had lost its respect—and maybe even need—for *innovation.* Not *creativity,* which seemed dilettante and floofy to me here, something I might comment on in a well-decorated home. And not *invention,* tied so closely to intellectual property rights and ownership and therefore, consumerism and entrepreneurialism. Both are prized and present. But innovation has been automated, assumed. As if the entire responsibility for bettering the way objects worked in our lives lay with those who made them for us.

I had been seeing for myself: Americans were sold truths with ease in Cambodia that turned out to be somewhat less so, and felt a privilege because of it more damaging than ignorance. Innovation had given way to complacency and righteousness, and that seemed dangerous. The question, *Is there a way this thing in front of me—this machine, this organization, this system—might work better?* had simply stopped being asked.

•     •     •

## My Very Favorite Girl

I sat on the bed and Maly came in to see what I was doing. What I was doing was downloading a recording of Chandara giving me a tour of the National Museum. I gave her the earphones so she could listen to her sister talk about Cambodian art and history.

She enjoyed it and wanted to hear more, so I found the recording of all the girls, together, singing the Cambodian National Anthem. She liked that too, but it was short, so I turned on one of my Khmer language lessons and for some reason she enjoyed this also. I handed her my MP3 player, which had the Khmer lessons on it, and she listened to it for two hours. I did not know why. Or OK, maybe I did: When I was trying to learn Khmer in Chicago all I could my hands on were some books intended for Khmer people to learn English, and I listened to them diligently for months in an attempt to reverse engineer me some language comprehension skills. Maly was also boy crazy, and possibly intrigued by David Smythe's British accent, so perhaps she wanted to listen to him talk.

Lili came in and plunked down on my bed to do her homework. Then Dina Sun came in and we sat giggling and laughing about boys and whiteness and fatness: She believed herself to be too dark, and her roommate to be too fat, and boys to be uninterested in her, see point one. To cheer herself, she picked up an English-to-Khmer phrasebook and started practicing her Khmer.

Within a matter of minutes, I was the only girl on the bed not studying Khmer.

Notice please that three Cambodian young women can lie together on a bed that I find way too small for just myself. I looked at them, comfortably sardined together on the bottom bunk, and appreciated each in turn. Maly's precision, inherited from her mother, a money-lender. Lili's easy laugh. Dina Sun's rare capacity for self-consciousness and criticality.

I tried hard not to have favorites. I was sure I was doing well in this regard, because every time I found out something new about someone it was so much more awesome than the last thing I found out about the last person. Technically, I suppose I was doing very poorly at this, because every second I had a totally new favorite girl.

That day I had scrolled through all of them, though. Every single one. Because the zine-making instruction had finally taken hold. There were finally enough girls that had made them and enjoyed them and shared them with other girls that girls were coming home from school early to study with me and making zines on their own and then bring them back to me to copy.

That day, five different girls had completed five different zines on their own. Five girls who hadn't had the chance to come and study with me directly. Five girls who just saw something sitting around the dorm and thought, *Hey, I can do that. I have something to say.* And then said it.

·　·　·

### Playboy vs. Punkboy

One night Jorani, a stunningly beautiful girl by all American standards but sort of just average by Cambodian, with long dark hair, a smooth small face, and an easy quick smile, asked me a question that came to define my work at the Euglossa Foundation Dormitory for University Women.

"What are Playboy and Punkboy?" She asked.

Playboy, of course, is the bunny-head logo of the world-renowned naked-boobies magazine, while Punkboy was a phrase that decorated a t-shirt one of the girls in the dorm owned, that featured a culture jam of the Playboy logo, except this bunny head had a pierced ear, and notably failed to wear a tie. The bunny image, this logo, was surprisingly popular with the girls, considering. By which I mean that the students who resided at Euglossa were particular about the symbols they adapted and the culture they supported. Still, the first large group of young women to live together in dedication to a social justice agenda flaunted advertising for light porn on notebooks, house shoes, and hair accoutrements. Someone was being taken advantage of here, for this to have happened. And it was not Hugh Hefner. These girls were resolutely moral and sang, sometimes, the national anthem to themselves in the shower. They thought Britney Spears slutty and boyfriends kind of a distraction. But bunnies were cute. What luck for the Playboy brand!

I found this jarring, incoherent, and reprehensible, but said not a word. The decades of poverty all of Cambodia has endured combined with the popular acceptance of sex tourism results in many Khmer women being taken sexual advantage of; at least these girls were merely advancing a popular symbol of this worldwide power dynamic, and not physically succumbing to it. At least, in other words, these girls had any shirts on at all.

Anyway, I was not in Cambodia to admonish what of their developing culture had already been rebuilt, however jankily, with tools scrounged from Western cast-offs. I was there to provide more tools. Which I had been doing for a couple weeks when Jorani asked: "What are Playboy and Punkboy?"

"Playboy," I explained without value judgment, "is a logo, a picture that symbolizes a business in the United States famous for making magazines with pictures of ladies without clothes."

"Why?" Jorani asked me. Maly, whipsmart, wanted to be the president of a bank, and Amoun, future lawyer, were also there. Both asked, "Why make a magazine like this?"

"That is a good question," I agreed. "Because you know how there is prostitution here?" I did not mean, in Cambodia. From our position on the third floor balcony, we could see the neighbors solicit for sex. "Because that is a way to make money? This magazine is the same. It might not be the best way, but people make money when they put it out. So people do it."

"So it is not good," they agreed.

Whether they liked it or not, however, this symbol had seeped into their lives, and permeated their culture: Their small, pro-girl, rights-based culture. "Well, it does exploit women," I told them. "A rich man started the company, and many men work there. The magazine does allow readers to view women as objects, not think of them as smart. But people like to read it, too. Women also work there. It does some good, but it also does bad."

With you I'll be honest: I don't personally mind Playboy Enterprises one whit, but in a decent and just society I wouldn't be faced with the social consequences of Playboy's jerky readership in the States, not to mention that I wouldn't have to be reminded of its existence daily by young feminists in Cambodia.

"And it is legal?" Amoun asked. Lawyers!

"That is tricky to answer," I had to say. "It is not good to exploit women. We are supposed to have equal economic opportunities for men and women in the U.S. We are supposed to have as many options for women to express themselves as men. But this magazine makes that difficult. Even so, making this magazine is legal."

"Why?" They demanded. Because when they were in positions to decide whether or not Cambodia should allow such things, they wanted to be ready.

But how was I supposed to respond? That even in the U.S. life isn't actually fair? "Sometimes the law allows you to do very small things that might not always be good," I explained. "Like it is legal to smoke, and drink alcohol. But these are not good for you."

"Hmmm," they said. They woke up around 5 every morning, did homework, chores, and attended classes seven days a week, and often didn't get to bed until midnight. There was no room, nor money, for vice in this lifestyle. We had barely wrapped our minds around the concept of fun.

"So what is Punkboy?" Jorani asked.

"OK." I began, taking a breath. "That shirt that says Punkboy is like a joke that is not so funny. It is a joke about Playboy, but punk might be difficult for you to understand. Punk is a group of people in the U.S., and all over the world, that does not like big companies. Like in music, for example. You know how Britney Spears mostly sings songs about boys? When really there are many other things to think about? Like cooking, or going to school, or politics? And she makes a bad role model for girls by only thinking about boys? Britney works for a big music company. That's why even though she lives in the U.S., and she has never been to Cambodia, and maybe has never even heard of it, you see pictures of her every day. A punk is someone who wants music to be different, to not be like that, so makes their own music. And maybe sings about boys, but maybe sings about politics, or cooking, or something else. And they don't just make music, they also make their own magazines, and books, and comics, and clothes. And sometimes they wear weird clothes, or have piercings. That picture on the shirt is a joke, because a punk would not support Playboy. It is a joke because it would not happen."

"Oh. But a punk is always a boy?" This from Jorani. I know it reads fake, as if I made it up to prove a point, but I didn't.

"No, many punks are boys, but there are punks that are girls, too. Girls that think boys get too much attention in society and want to make their own things instead of buying things boys make. And support each other in making girl things."

I did not say the name, riot grrrl. Because they would say to me, *revolution is bad.* This was still Cambodia.

"Oh. Creative," Amoun said. She said it like this: *Cree. Ay. Tiv.* "Like you." She put her fingers to her eyebrow and pinched. It was a reference to my eyebrow ring.

"So can anyone be punk?" Jorani asked.

"Yes," I said. "Anyone. It is not a club you have to join, but you also do not have to use that name. You can want those things, but not call yourself punk. You do not have to wear different clothes or have a weird piercing. You can just make your own stuff."

"Like what?" Jorani wanted to know.

"Well, you can make your own little book, like we made this morning in my class." *Gkon sieuw poav* was the term we used for zines—the word *zine* was catching on, English pronunciation, but usage was complicated by the fact that it's not in dictionaries.

Jorani had missed my class that morning: She was studying I.T. and several languages so could not fit in extra projects. "If you cannot come to my class," I told her, "I can show you how to make one."

"OK." She said. "We can make one now?"

"We can," I said.

So the happy ending to that day was that we all went off to my dorm room to make zines.

•    •    •

## The Advantage of Dorm

I had been helping the girls with midterms, which were coming up for almost all of them, and which are usually taught in English. Although many university classes are also taught in English, and the girls take supplementary language lessons in the dorm and in school, few are taught by native speakers. Mistakes in pronunciation become entrenched, idioms translated directly, little cultural context provided. Consequently, a great mystery surrounds the language, and even those who have lucked into a near-perfect grasp of it pose staunch declarations as unsteady questions.

Poor Amara just couldn't feel comfortable speaking the foreign tongue, could barely say "hello, sister," after a year of study. We communicated mostly via the language of hugging.

Someone else had to tell me how Amara had come to live at Euglossa. The quiet, sweet creature had simply shown up on the Phnom Penh doorstep of a funder some weeks following the unofficially leaked announcement of a potential new university scholarship.

"The scholarship wasn't even in place at the time!" The funder herself told me. She was American, and lived in that other Phnom Penh, the wealthy ex-pat city that floated somewhere above the Cambodia I knew. "It had really only been a rumor!"

Amara spoke not a word of English at the time. This annoyed the donor, who despite having owned a residence in the country for years had never learned Khmer. But the girl was so eager—and smart—that her parents had brought her out from their home in the provinces to the funder's city abode in the family oxcart. They refused to leave until someone interviewed the girl for the position, in case it became available.

"Country people," the donor ended the tale, as if the proper procedure in this situation had been ignored. She waved her fingers dismissively. "What are you going to do?" she asked. She looked burdened.

Amara was given a scholarship, and when the Euglossa dorm opened, she moved in. Amara didn't need language to communicate.

But she and her sisters wanted help with their midterms. Usually in the Cambodian educational system, these are offered in the form of take-home essays on key elements in the student's field of study, almost universally following the assignment format: *An Essay on the Advantages and Disadvantages of [Insert Topic Here]*.

In the Khmenglish we spoke at Euglossa, however, this was shortened to: *The Advantage and Disadvantage of [Subject]*. This configuration made it easier to sneak into conversation. It could then be made to appear as if we were just chatting over breakfast and not drafting homework assignments. As if I would not notice if I were asked over coffee to please address the advantage and disadvantage of privatized health insurance while everyone took notes, for example, or, the advantage and disadvantage of democracy. One particularly cruel assignment was the midterm essay on the advantage and disadvantage of girls in higher education. So when I casually asked my students in writing class one day to please jot me a short paragraph on what they'd learned about self-publishing and distribution, I received in response thirty-two essays titled *The Advantage and Disadvantage of Zine.*

A few days later, I lectured at a local university on journalism, self-publishing, and marketing. I spoke, as I have in cities around the world, on my own history in the cultural underground of North America, as a young woman in a boycentric culture, as a person who engaged in media creation and criticism not to make money at it, but as an act of survival. I worked in self-publishing as an effort to see myself reflected in the culture I intended to live in, and so that accurate stories about people like me could be told. Most of what I created, I gave away for free. This was not an act of marketing; this was how I expressed my desire to communicate. I tied this to my experiences at Euglossa, and discussed the self-publishing work we had been doing there for the last few months. I was desperate for my audience to connect with these messages, to take them home and do with them whatever they would. I passed around how-to zines, in Khmer and English, and talked about how easy it was. Shared exampled of others who self-published, what they made. Why.

"It is a good idea," one attendee commented during the Q and A session after my talk. "To have a place to express your own idea."

"Thank you," I said. "But I did not invent it."

Apparently, however, the healthy dose of finer points about living in a community of highly educated young Cambodian women also took hold in my audience. Implying that I had waxed somewhat overpoetic on a controversial subject, I was asked next, "Please to comment also on the *Disadvantage* of Dorm."

So.

.    .    .

## The Disadvantage of Dorm

My roommate Amoun had watched me intently that day as I put on makeup before the lecture. Professors at universities in Cambodia—any professionals, really, in any field, as well as anyone in any service position whatsoever—dress for success. This was not a manner of presentation I was well-suited to. Quite literally: I had purchased my fell-off-the-truck Gap t-shirt for $2 U.S. at the market and a wraparound skirt for $4 in Siem Reap, just a few steps up even from my usual tank-and-whatever-I-slept-in warm weather fare. Makeup application is not a natural part of my skillset either, as for some reason I go spasmodic when opening mascara. Professional attire always feels like full-fledged drag to me.

Amoun was one of the most beautiful humans I had ever laid eyes on: Long dark hair, twinkling eyes, a serene poise. In her presence I could look like nothing but a vaguely femininized blob of goo. When she first approached me at the door of the dormitory months ago, I did not fully comprehend at the time that four of us would share a room together the size of my bedroom at home. That Cambodian women enrolled at university wake up at an unholy hour to prepare for school. That for the next few months I would understand very little of what was said out loud. Except the giggling. She sat then about three feet away from me and watched as I negotiated the demands of the local dress code.

I don't know that it's all that unusual to be nervous when people watch you do normal stuff; surveillance implies scrutiny, judgment. Perhaps it was uniquely American for me to suggest that Amoun perhaps had something more productive she could be doing with her time. She didn't. Watching me was it. At the Euglossa Dormitory for University Women at 8 in the morning, if you don't have class that day, the electricity is out, and your schoolwork is already completed because you are a diligent student, I was the most entertaining thing going. I did my hair. Amoun watched. I looked at her. And applied some lotion. Amoun watched this, too. I looked at her again.

"Does it make you shy when I watch you?" She asked. As if there were more than one answer possible.

"Yes," I told her. "I mean, I'm a fairly shy person anyway." This is still true. Apparently, however, I am most shy when people watch intently as I pick at my face.

"Why?" She asked. The scrutiny was not just physical. These were questions about self-image, and culture.

"Because most of the time, I do not have people watch me do things. Remember, I do not live with thirty-two girls at home. Just my cat, and he thinks I am very boring, unless I am feeding him. And in big cities like Chicago, people do not pay attention to each other. Does that make sense?"

"Yes," she said. "It is a very good reason. At my home, my family watches me do everything. All the time."

It was true. At home she had two brothers and two parents and many cats and an entire farm full of animals, and they shared a small house on stilts and she had never had a secret. Her rituals for dressing without flashing skin were elaborate; when she had a thought perhaps best kept to herself she expressed it. When she had a thought certainly best left unexpressed, she trained her mind not to think it again. As much as I think, *Hey. It must suck to grow up with no privacy,* I also think, *It is no wonder you are so confident. It is no wonder you pop out of bed every morning happy and dance a rock-and-roll Apsara, or that you stand in a crowded room and hula hoop like it's normal to move so freely, or that you sing the national anthem to yourself in the shower.*

It was hard for me to live with someone watching me all the time, but for her this was just how love worked.

6

## WHAT IS SUPPOSED TO BE GRATIFYING

• • •

*It is One Thing to Teach About Zines in Cambodia, But it is Another to Teach About Them to the Illiterate and Hearing Impaired*
Not that it is impossible, exactly, but when I was asked to give an hour-long workshop on self-publishing to an organization that works with former child sex workers, I was excited, but not about the product: I didn't care what their stories were. If you are a former child sex worker, it is amazing what I will let you get away with in the guise of *self-publishing*. I don't even want you to feel beholden to being honest with me, to writing or drawing or folding or photocopying. *Whatever is cool.* You just get your shit out however you need to.

A self-publishing workshop, however, does rely on certain commonalities. Like a knowledge of, umm, books. Basic language skills. Literacy. Some shared form of communication that does not need to be verbal. In an educational setting, even if you speak only Khmer and I speak only English, maybe it will be OK, because at least you can hear me, and probably we can find a way to gesture. A little bit. Somehow. I had become moderately skilled at body language, and had built a moderate vocabulary. *This will be fine,* I thought.

Yet as the workshop started, I was fed the news: Oh, some of these girls cannot hear or speak. Most of them cannot read or write a single word, in any language.

Which might have been information I could have used to plan for the workshop, that, by the way, I prepared in mangled Khmer. For real. I finally got on top of the language enough to use it, at the same exact moment I'd found a community that had little use for it.

I was thrown. A roomful of former child sex workers have a desperate need to please, but I could communicate almost nothing. A sweet and kind translator, an older male, however, helped very little: No one appeared comfortable with him, nor were they versed in the Khmer sign language he was prepared to use. Any commonalities I had forged with other young Cambodian women were not here apparent. I panicked and contemplated my own hubris: *Who the hell did I think I was to come here?* I flushed in the intolerable mid-day heat, but also with anger.

I'd scaled back my expectations for the workshop to almost nothing. What I'd wanted when I walked into the room was to fold some paper with some kids and fill the resultant little booklets with something. Anything. Twenty minutes in, we'd made no progress. Moreover, I could no longer perceive a single reason how a workshop on independent media making would ever, *ever*, be worthwhile to an impoverished and abused girl who could not hear or speak or write. I had never in my life felt so useless. The great empty void of my experience, knowledge, supposed expertise . . . it did me no good. Now what I wanted from the workshop experience was to survive it.

A roomful of young people brimming with hope looked at me. Former child sex workers in Cambodia are shockingly hip dressers. One wore a tie, another a jaunty vest. Head scarves were involved. Layers. They were not as touchy-feely with each other as the young women I lived with, and who could blame them. I had seen documentaries about the kinds of experiences they might have had, situations where the word "rape" stands in as a pleasant euphemism for the incomprehensible abuse and degradation that really goes down. If even an image from one floated into my consciousness my throat caught. *I should leave*, I thought. I closed my eyes.

I started over.

"Here," I said, in English, picking up the piece of A4. It didn't matter if I communicated anything, I decided. It only mattered that they see me wanting to try. "Fold it in half, like a hot dog." They would never have had a hot dog, would not know it from an entire side of beef, and what sense would that have made, *Fold it in half like a side of beef*? I was talking eighteen kinds of nonsense, in a language they did not speak. But I meant it.

"Then fold it again, like this." I showed them. "Then unfold it, and refold it, but this time, like a hamburger." *Why. The. Fuck.* The metaphors are stupid enough if you understand them; the process nonsensical unless you're familiar with its purpose. "Then cut this part here." I exaggerated my actions dramatically, and as I did, looked up to see one girl in the back of the room picking up a pair of scissors.

"Then unfold it." I opened up the piece of paper. Mostly blank expressions I couldn't meet considered me as I scanned quickly for comprehension. "Look, it should have a slit, right in the middle." I held it on both sides, above my head, like a protestor at a rally against pieces of paper that did not have slits down the middle.

"Then, refold it. Like this. That's when the fun begins." I waited, musing on that meaningless word, fun.

A cry of anger from the girl in the back, a rustling. She had cut the wrong edge, and crinkled the useless piece of paper into a ball. It is rare to be so angry at something here that you can discern no future potential use for it, and discard. These girls knew that better than most.

This young woman was deaf, and said something I could not understand, but the girl next to her helped refold and recut. When the first girl opened up the piece of A4 this time, slit down the very center of the paper, she bolted straight up out of her seat. She screamed. The entire room cheered. It was like a football game in a movie.

Except one where, at the end of the movie, the crowd starts playing football too. The roomful of former child sex workers—a respectful term that feigns a complicity on the part of the very young I wasn't sure could be applied here—suddenly got it. Got. It. One hearing-impaired girl drew a picture of a flower on every page of her zine. Then she flipped through it for me, narrating a story I could not understand, beaming. Another girl—the tie-wearing snappy dresser—drew clever outfits on stick figures. All the girls wore ties. A zine about a happy family, another only landscapes. Far away landscapes. Nothing you could see in the city.

And the only one with any text at all, translated into English with the help of the translator, titled: *My Dream of Life When I am Rich.* Months later I stumble across a photograph of it and sob uncontrollably for hours. This was the only time I allow myself to shed tears about Cambodia's past.

.      .      .

## The Part of Teaching That's Supposed to Be Gratifying

Sotheary finished a zine and went off and copied it at the Minotal copyshop. She handed me one from a stack about thirty-five high. It was a story about the history of Phnom Penh. I had no idea she was working on it.

The last page of her zine explains that she is proud to have been able to tell to you the history of her adopted city in zine form, but that many Cambodian people are not able to read or write. Sotheary writes that you are lucky to be able to do both. She'd like to know what you think of this situation. Here is her email address.

What she did not explain was that she had translated the history of Phnom Penh from a Khmer text, which took about a week and a half, since Khmer-English dictionaries are dicey at best, and there were only a few in the dorm. Sotheary was 19.

I was proud and I was thrilled. I no longer needed to explain every step of the process. It was theirs already. I did not need to ask if they had learned anything. They had, and used, all the tools they needed to publish the information they deemed important in the world, whether in English or in Khmer, or whatever other languages they wanted. And I had seen them use these tools when they felt they had something to say.

I had come to see if I could teach them a skill. And now they possessed that skill. That's the part about teaching we're supposed to find gratifying, but I don't know. It was also very, deeply sad. The girls at Euglossa no longer needed me.

•   •   •

## Distribution

I dragged Narin and Sotheary with me nearly kicking and screaming to the bookstore to drop off more zines, because I wanted them to be able to distribute them after I was gone, and anyway they had never been there and rarely go anywhere besides their school so, new place! Also, they should see how excited people get about their zines! As I had suspected, the last batch of zines was thoroughly gone. When we walked into the bookstore, the woman I'd handed the last batch to was very excited to see us.

"I tried to email you!" She said. "But at this email address!" And she showed me someone else's email address. "I did not think it is yours because this is a Khmer name!" She said.

So I gave her my correct email address and I introduced the girls and then we dropped off more zines. Narin and Sotheary asked a few shy questions about who was taking them, and whether people liked them, and what exactly was sold in this store. We were given a small tour. Narin asked who shopped there (mostly foreigners), how many books they had, and what it was like to see so many books every day. It started to become clear that she'd never been in a bookstore before. One that offers books that are published, officially, and legally, by people who did not also write, design, and illustrate them. And has doors! Book stands, with used or pirated books, can be found in tourist areas. Or giant stacks of blue-inked collections of aphorisms and instructions in markets. Young people on the street sell books out of bins Kroma-ed around their necks, tragic books about evil to travelers who come here to smell blood. Even after months in a largely illiterate culture, I was shocked to realize that bookstores were not universal.

This one had a small café in the back, so I asked if my companions wanted something to eat. Confusingly, the word *snack* is pronounced by the girls like the word *snake*. Our conversation went like this:

Narin and Sotheary: "Yes, we want a snake."

Me: "You are disgusting, why would you want that?"

Narin and Sotheary: "You asked!"

Me: "We don't have time for animals. I meant, like, a brownie."

Which you might think would clear things up but since they had never had one actually didn't.

We asked for two cookies and a brownie. While they prepared our order, the Khmer staff of the café talked to them in some detail in Khmer about the foods they served there and the people who came there, some of whom were white and British and talking on the couch in front of us. The girls were quiet. They were in foreign space, in a space meant for foreigners, and one they had never imagined before, but they learned: This was not only their country and their town, but now a place for them. They fit in. They made things you could find here. They were integral. And so in their shyness they sat, backs straight, on the edge of the couch. Politely, but also to be noticed. The staff did, and brought them a special water jug, asked how they were enjoying themselves; if they were happy.

They were happy, but still uncomfortable. Also, they had never had a brownie, which I imagine for them would be something like if I admitted I had never ridden a water buffalo. Thank the Buddha this place served the kind with frosting on it and that they heated it up and then topped it with whipped cream. So the girls learned what, in the future, to demand of their brownies. It was still hard to sell them on this new thing.

"Have some brownie," I told them. "You will want it to be your new boyfriend."

"Is it good?" They asked.

It was very good, but I do not want to oversell it. "Just try it," I said. "If you do not think it is good, I will eat it all."

So Narin and Sotheary each took a bite, and smiled widely.

"This is probably the most important aspect of self-publishing," I said.

They giggled. They probably thought I was lying.

•       •       •

*Kimlong*

Kimlong pretended she did not speak English very well so she did not have to explain how smart she was to other people. She would prefer just to *be* smart, off on her own. Last night she asked if it would be OK if she wrote a story about what the Khmer Rouge were like in her village before she was born, but also as she was growing up, and whether if she sent it to me for editing and grammar I could help her. I suddenly realized how closely she paid attention. To me, to her surroundings. Which wasn't even the best part. The best part was when she asked me if she could take some more copies of the Khmer-language translation of the how-to guide I'd made, *How to Make This Very Zine*. She wanted to bring them back to her home village, because she thought the children there would be interested to learn how to make zines.

"They like to paint and draw," she said. "But they do not have much opportunity."

For some weeks, with the girls' permission, I had been copying and mailing zines back to the States—to zinesters, libraries, artists, friends, teachers, comics creators. The girls had begun to get emails back from their new fans on the other side of the world. They were seeing that their thoughts, drawings, observations, and love for Cambodia were being taught in college classrooms, displayed in museums, integrating into book-lending facilities, and re-photocopied and re-distributed around New York, Rhode Island, California, Texas, Illinois, and Wisconsin. They had begin to feel pride in their stake in the world.

Kimlong wanted to make sure that, once she taught the children in her home village how to make zines, I would help her send them out to people. Around the U.S., or the world.

"Of course," I said.

"I think it good," she said, "that people know about the real Cambodia."

"I think it good too," I told her. "The real Cambodia is an amazing place."

•     •     •

## Leung Reads a Map

The site of Gold Tower 42—it is true that there are two towers, but sometimes we drop S's, you know—is a few short kilometers north of the Euglossa Dormitory for University Women. Leung and I walked toward it from the dorm on a Tuesday afternoon.

We were headed toward Psar Toul Tom Poung and instead of taking transportation like a moto because she is Cambodian, we took walking because I claimed I wanted to exercise even though really I just like walking. Americans do, and Cambodians think it is crazy. But it allows you to say "Hello!" to people, and take pictures of carnival rides, and find a small thing on the ground that people think is garbage even though it is beautiful.

To walk to this market from the dorm, you need to use a map, and you need to use it well. The streets in Phnom Penh are not always labelled, and the houses are not in order, and I can tell you from experience that between the dorm and the market there was not a single labeled street, anywhere along the way. And anyway there was always an interesting dog or machine gun on the way to distract you, and it wasn't like you could ask anyone how to walk to the market, even in Khmer. Because walking places is crazy. And that's what they would tell you.

So although it was mostly a straight line from the dorm to the market, there was a detour I liked to take. It went by a janky, run-down carnival that featured rides so rusted and creaking they didn't even look enjoyable anymore—just terrifying—and where the gravel was embedded with shattered balloons. It was sublime and quiet, like the site of a child's tragic death. Leung was not impressed. Everywhere she goes was the likely site of a real child's tragic death. We continued on toward the market.

We got turned around. I told Leung, casually, "Oh, I do not know where we are." At the same moment, she looked up in front of her and I looked down to my side: She was looking around for someone to ask where to go, and I was pulling out my map. An object she found a little intriguing but mostly boring. She hadn't seen one before.

"This is a map, a picture of the city," I told her. "We can use it to find where we are. Here is a drawing of the street we are on. See?"

You could see her studying the clean line drawing and thinking, *That is not what it looks like here. That creek, which is really raw sewage, is not blue. This doesn't make sense.*

Leung was a deeply intelligent girl with a lovely singing voice. She adored her mother and her grandmother, and living away from them in the dorm was hard. She was the youngest of the Euglossa girls, and primed for frustration in a way Cambodians tend not to be. In a country rampant with corruption, tolerant of a Prime Minister with direct ties to the Khmer Rouge, where food, gas, and water are sometimes simply too expensive to purchase and so you did without them, and where the privilege of something like stress reduction techniques are impossible to conceive of, patience was common. But Leung would fly to fury, yell, storm out of rooms. She would make jokes about cutting, walk away, refuse to engage. Ignore you. She was difficult. It was true. But she was also one of the only girls at Euglossa ready and equipped to demand something better. Unwilling to stand for a mere symbol of progress, an abstraction of a path to success: She was deeply skeptical of my map. She wanted to be at her destination.

But this map was the kind of thing that could help her. "Look, you can think about this situation in a removed way," I told her. "Here, we can float above it all and decide which way to go. The options are here, in front of us. This is sort of what they look like. Do you see this building? On the map it looks like this. And here is a picture of where we are going. What path should we take to get there?"

So Leung navigated the rest of the walk with the map. We held hands, because this was what girls did in Cambodia, and she taught me how to say, *Will you hold hands with me?* in Khmer. I said it loudly, and in a funny voice, so I would remember it. Everyone who passed by us thought I was, you know, not very bright, possibly even mentally underdeveloped. Oh well. At least Leung learned how to read a map.

And she asked me questions about maps. "Where is dorm?" She started.

"Down at the bottom," I showed here. "Here."

"And the skyscraper?"

"Right over there. Look, it will be visible soon, far above that building." I pointed in front of us.

"Is this how come you feel safe going places alone, even though you are a woman?"

"Yes, Leung," I said. "Partially."

"But what if you come to a bad neighborhood?" She asked.

"I know some self-defense," I told her.

"What is self-defense?" she wanted to know.

"Oh my gosh," I told her, "That is a good question."

So we walked hand-in-hand to the market and talked about protecting yourself and feeling safe and strong alone in a big city that doesn't seem to care about you. In a developing country that has no idea what you are capable of.

## EPILOGUE

•　　　•　　　•

*Essay Assignment: Tell Me What You Think About Zines*

### THE ADVANTAGE OF MAKING A ZINE
By Dina Sun

ZINE is self publish periodical that is created of the passion and do not for profit. There are several advantages of ZINE. First, making zine makes us very happy and we can write and draw whatever I want. For example, I have made a zine about the pretty countryside. And the second is we can educate or provide out ideas by the zine. . . . Finally, we can know a lot of friends by the zine. Example, I have just known some new friends. They read my zine and the mailed me, so I'm very happy. In conclusion. . . . I am very enjoy making the zine so much.

### THE ADVANTAGE AND DISADVANTAGE OF SELF-PUBLISHING
By Narin

I think that SELF-PUBLISHING it nice Because I can draw a picture what I want or what I think I want to say I can write with a good picture it look nice. Anyway it make me feel better from debressed Because it look funny. . . . I want all person start to do it.

### THE ADVANTAGE OF ZINE
By Maly

. . . The title of my zine is "Ratanakiri." I told you about the population and their jobs, resort, and the ethnic groups. I am really interested in making zines. Now, I would like to tell you the advantages of the zine. . . . :
   • It is a new thing for everybody and it is so interesting.

- We can know how to make a zine and draw picture in it.
- If we want to advertise something, we can use a zine as well
- If we want to let somebody or introduce ourself we also can use a zine too.
- Now, we know how to make, and if there is someone to talk about zine we will have a lot of ideas to share with them.

Thank you!

## THE ADVANTAGES AND DISADVANTAGES OF ZINES
### By Sosaryna

. . . I have been making a zine, one is about "how to coin" and another is about "my place of birth." I will continue to do and make other zines in order to show my ideas and my identity. Making zine is wonderfull. We can impresss what we want people to know. It is very small so we can pact it everywhere and sometime we can put it in someone pocket to let them see or wonder or surprise. We can write or draw anything we want to do and we can give it to anyone we want to give. It's very cheap to make a zine, just a sheet of A4 paper and a pen. . . .

## HELLO! MY NAME CHANDARA
### By Chandara

. . . I like to make a sine and I already did it. . . . It is easy to make a zine and zine make me happy when I draw the picture and write some things that I want people to know. When I fell bored I make zine ad it make me more creation and happier and have a lot of imagine. In the future I will use it (the zine) to communicate with another person I can show my idea to the peoples and let them know a lot of information that I wrote in the zine such as I wrote about my country, traditional, people, environment and another thing. Anyway, I will let my friend make the zine and when they already make they can give them to me or another people so we can know each other. . . . Comic is very lovely for me.

## HOLLE! HOW ARE YOU?
### By Kimlong

I'm very happy that I have chance to study, how to do zine! . . . Before I never see and learn how to draw at all. This is my first draw, it's not beautiful. Zine can make flexible to think what we should do or draw for somebody to know from our mind and our thinking when we draw although it's so short. When we get bore or unhappy with something or somebody, we can make it and write a short fun. I think, we'll get better. . . .

## THE ADVANTAGE AND DISADVANTAGE OF SELF-PUBLISHING
### By Jorani

I think that when I study with Anne about SELF-PUBLISHING I think that it can help me paint the picture on the papers. . . . You know I never draw the picture because in the countryside don't has people—want to draw and some students or peoples never think about it in the school for the child or primary school should make this subject. I like draw picture now. If all student know about self-publishing we can make the book for the people all on the world now and can help your country.

•     •     •

*Emailing From the U.S. with Chenda*
Dear Sister Anne,
You know, on 3rd of March, I am doing a presentation about show and tell. It means I have to bring one object and then I have to show to my classmates and explain them about that object. I am going to show my friends about zine but I am not sure whether I can do it well or not, because I think I don't know about zine. Is it OK if I do a presentation about a zine? Can you give me the definition of zine? Can you give three important reasons of making a zine? I have tried to check dictionary to find this word yet I cannot find it. I know the advantages of it. However, I want to get the correct information from you because you are the one who expert at zine.
     Love,
     Your Sister Chenda

Dear Chenda,

I highly encourage you to do a presentation about zine! In my opinion it is the funnest thing you can do a presentation about. Since you know already what a zine looks like, and how to make one, I can tell you how I define zine: It is a hand-made booklet, created by only one person or a small group of people, that is not intended to forward a business or make money.

I think it is important to make a zine because I think everyone should be able to decide what a very small part of the world looks like. I think it is important to have a place to freely express all of your ideas, even if you can never say them out loud, and even if you do not show them to anybody. But there are lots of people who are expert in zine besides me, so I asked two friends why they think it's important to make a zine.

My friend Kevin Dunn in Geneva, NY publishes a zine called *Geneva13* with poems, drawings, essays, photos, and other contributions from a variety of people, most of whom live in Geneva, New York. He started it because he wanted the people of his town to have a place where they could express their thoughts and creativity, a place where we as a community could reflect on who we are and what we hope to be. Each issue is about 60 pages long. He gives them out for free, and prints between 500 and 600 of every one. He is also a professor of political science and a father of two young daughters. His three important reasons for making a zine were:

> 1) It is important for people to be able to express themselves, their opinions, and their creative voices. The more voices that can be heard in the world, the more beautiful the music will be that we all make.
> 2) It is very empowering. Most publications are geared towards selling you something, making you a passive consumer. But by being a zine-maker, you become an active producer of ideas and culture.
> 3) It keeps your mind sharp, agile and creative. As we get older, we tend to lose the creative playfulness that we had as children. Making zines is one way to keep ourselves grounded in creativity.
> And (4) because zine-makers are cool people and making zines puts you into contact with cool people all over the world, like you!

My other friend, R. John Xerxes wrote:
There are so many more reasons to make a zine than just three!

1) IT IS FUN TO MAKE A ZINE!!! This is really the best possible reason to make a zine! Making a zine is like art projects, you get to play with scissors, glue, crayons, markers, all sorts of cool things. In your zine you can make collages, draw pictures, write stories, and basically anything else you want to do!

2) It is fun to share your zine with people! Once you have made your zine, giving it to other people is almost as much fun as making it! Sharing your ideas, pictures, and stories might make someone else happy, or better yet, it might help someone else to want to make their own zine. Trading zines with other people who make them is one of the best joys of making zines, because I always love to see what other people make and write. Plus I learn so many different things. When someone talks about a passion or love, these are the best conversations I have had. After reading one of these zines, I always want to make my own zine. Other people's zines inspire me to make my own zines!

3) Zines are a great way to make friends! Zines are like pen pal letters to people you do not know! Zines let you tell other people all about your life, where you live, how you live, and everything else! Sometimes, the people who read the zine you make, write back to you and tell you about themselves or what they liked in your zine. Then you have new friends! Plus if you make your zine about local events, ideas, bands, people, then other people around you might see that you like the same things as they do!

So Chenda, here is a little bit more information for you. But remember that you are also expert in zine, so whatever you say or think about zine is OK to tell the students in your show and tell presentation.

Good luck and please let me know how it went! I miss you very much.
Heart,
Your Sister Anne

Dear Sister,
Hello sister! How are you? I miss you very much. You know this afternoon I did a presentation about show and tell. I got successful with my show and everyone in my class were very interested in making zine very much. You see, when I said that I would like to show you one special object and it is called zine, everyone in my class were very surprised and their face seemed very strange and they paid attention to listen to me and asked me a lot of questions. After I finished my show, my classmates asked me to see zine and they try to check it whether they can make it or not. One of question including who taught me how to make a zine and I told them "I got from Anne Alizabeth Moore." I am really happy today because I have done my show successfully and I can make other people be interested in making zine.

Thank you very much for kindness to give me lots of fantastic details about zine. Goodbye!!!

Heart,
Chenda

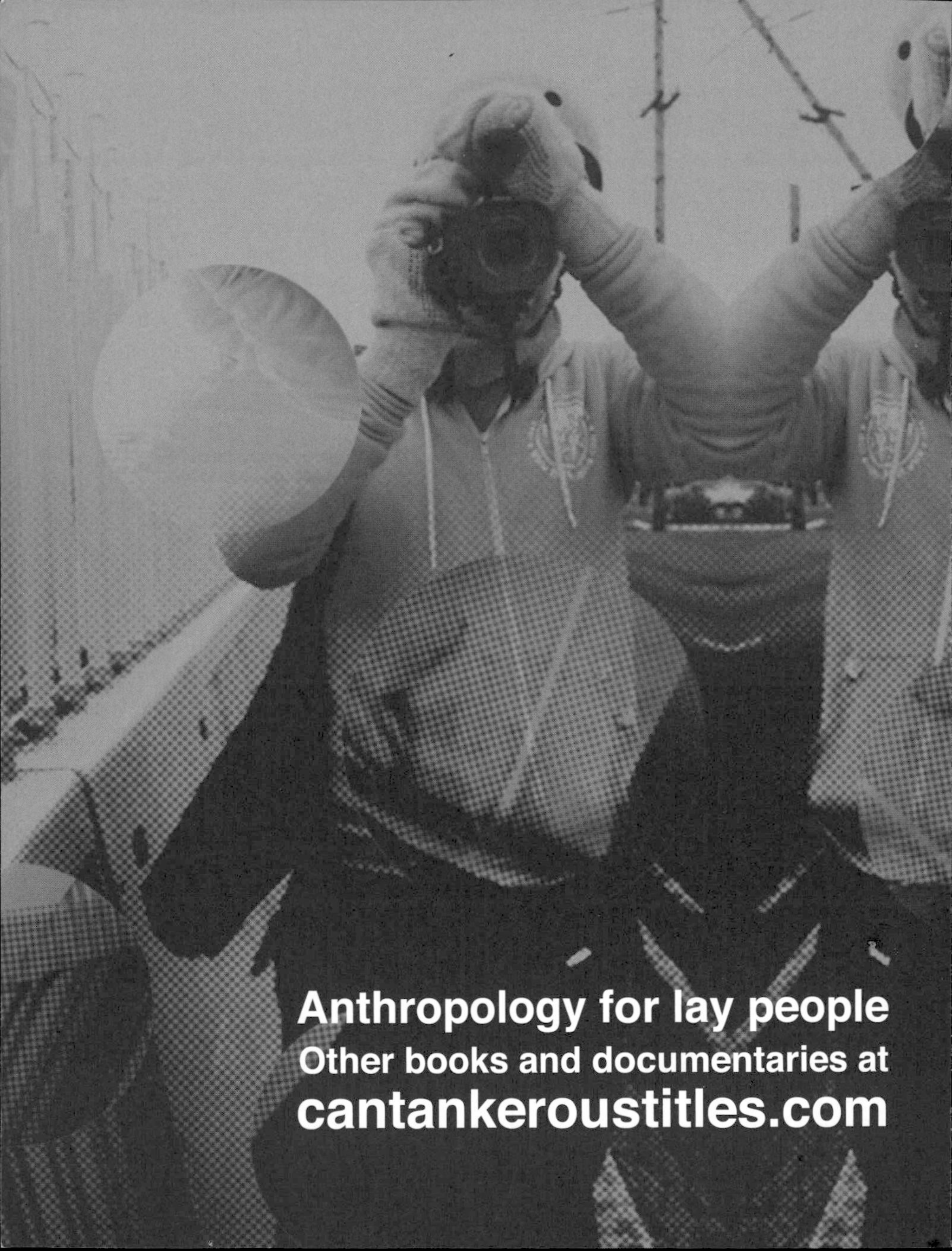
Anthropology for lay people
Other books and documentaries at
cantankeroustitles.com